Presented to:

....

From:

....

Date:

....

Watching
- in -
Wonder

GROWING IN FAITH DURING
YOUR BABY'S FIRST YEAR

A Devotional Journal

CATHERINE CLAIRE LARSON

THOMAS NELSON
Since 1798

Watching in Wonder

Published in Nashville, Tennessee, by Thomas Nelson. Thomas Nelson is a registered trademark of HarperCollins Christian Publishing, Inc.

Published in association with The Bindery Agency, www.TheBinderyAgency.com.

Thomas Nelson titles may be purchased in bulk for educational, business, fund-raising, or sales promotional use. For information, please email SpecialMarkets@ThomasNelson.com.

Any internet addresses, phone numbers, or company or product information printed in this book are offered as a resource and are not intended in any way to be or to imply an endorsement by Thomas Nelson, nor does Thomas Nelson vouch for the existence, content, or services of these sites, phone numbers, companies, or products beyond the life of this book.

ISBN 978-1-4002-3618-3 (audiobook)
ISBN 978-1-4002-3617-6 (eBook)
ISBN 978-1-4002-3610-7 (HC)

Printed in India

23 24 25 26 27 BPI 10 9 8 7 6 5 4 3 2 1

To my sons, Luke, Isaiah, James, Beau, David, and Elijah:
May you grow into mighty men of God.

Contents

Introduction

◇◇◇◇◇◇◇◇◇◇◇◇◇◇◇◇◇◇◇◇◇◇◇◇◇◇◇◇◇◇◇◇◇

Beholding and Becoming

Nothing compares to that first moment you hold your wriggling, warm baby in your arms. The exhilaration and pure delight are unlike anything else you will ever feel. By the kindness and mercy of God, I've experienced this six times, and I can tell you, it never gets old. Aside from my wedding day, these are the six best moments in my life so far.

Having had the privilege of walking this road before, I can testify that it's a time of strenuous demands on our bodies and hearts. Every new child has brought a period of disequilibrium (like that dizzy feeling you get after riding a roller coaster) as I've adjusted to the new demands of adding another soul to our family. Whether you're welcoming your first baby or your fifth, it can be difficult to maintain regular, close, daily time with God with everything off balance: our routines, hormones, emotions—in short, our normal. Regaining both our balance and regular time spent in the Word can be challenging.

As disorienting as the first year can be, it is also a time of rare beauty and wonder. There is nothing quite as breathtaking as a newborn: a new life, a new soul, a beautiful possibility whose days are yet unwritten. Like that roller coaster that takes your breath away, that first year—and the swift pace at which your little one develops—is unlike any other point in their lives. First smiles, first laughs, first scoots and crawls melt your heart. This amazing life blossoming in front of your eyes is no accident, but a carefully and thoughtfully designed creation of God. God has given *you* the incredibly high and holy calling of motherhood. Whether you are crossing the motherhood threshold for the very first time or approaching it again, your charge is no less sacred. You have been called to mother this beautiful child: to pray over, to cherish, and to nurture this incredible trust given to you.

These days deserve remembering. Despite all the challenges, take the time to record those fleeting glimpses of wonder that lead us back to the heart of God. Record the prayers that set the tone for your child's life. You will cherish these. Finally, lean into your God-given calling of motherhood, a mission of incredible importance.

While you are watching in wonder as that little marvel develops before your eyes, I want to lead you to also watch with equal wonder the ways of your God. Each week, I will share one characteristic of the Father, Son, or Holy Spirit upon which you can meditate. I want you to, in the words of that wonderful, old hymn "Turn Your Eyes Upon Jesus," "look full in His wonderful face." These are the days we hold our little ones in our arms, admiring every facet and detail of them—watching them, cherishing them, beholding them. It is with this same feeling of awe and wonder that I want to lead you to God within these devotionals. As the psalmist David wrote, "My heart says to you, 'Your face, Lord, do I seek'" (Psalm 27:8 esv). What would it mean to spend a year marveling at the face of God? What a beautiful way to begin your calling to mother this particular child.

For moms of infants, the days (and nights) can be full. We don't have the luxury of much quiet time or even alone time. We learn to fit it in when and where we can. For me, many a nursing session has become prayer time. While washing dishes, I often meditate on a single verse of Scripture thoughtfully and prominently placed at the window over the sink. Coffee and Bible go hand in hand. And when I haven't been able to balance both my gigantic study Bible and an infant, reading the Word on an e-reader or phone works in a pinch. I've learned to feed my soul through worship music or a Christian podcast while folding laundry or taking the baby for a walk. In short, as moms, we must be creative and snatch time with Jesus whenever and wherever we can.

In consideration of the busyness of new mothers' lives, I formatted this devotional journal carefully so that it's not too much and yet just enough. I provide three devotional entries and one journaling opportunity each week. I hope you'll meditate on the theme of the week, that specific attribute of God, regardless of whether you find time to read every devotional or write every journal entry. However you carve out your time to use this devotional journal, please feel the freedom: this devotional is an invitation, not a shackle.

For the newborn weeks, I offer week-by-week guides on your baby's development. As your baby grows, those switch to monthly summaries. At the end of each month are pages for recording those baby milestones you don't want to forget. But again, if those pages don't all get filled, don't stress, Mama—chances are you were busy rocking a baby or looking into those dear little eyes. Your heart will be full, even if there are empty pages in this book! Either way, I hope the devotions will be an encouragement to your soul.

The first year of your infant's life will be full of wonderful moments: from first snuggles and smiles to those adorable, if not clumsy, attempts your baby makes to sit without toppling over to messy experiments with solid foods. While your wonder and awe of your constantly changing little one grows, I hope your heart also grows in gratitude for our unchanging God. As you study every little detail of the babe in your arms, from that dimpled chin down to those kissable toes, I hope you'll also be drawn to notice the nuances of our God and worship the One who created and sustains that little wonder.

So put up your feet for a moment, dear Mama, and let's take a few minutes together to enjoy the wonder of God and this new little life given to you. The year will go fast, but God has called us to seize and savor the day.

Note: Dear reader, you are so unique and so is your baby. Please forgive me that I cannot write to every situation—the adopting mama, the mom of a special-needs child, the mom of multiples, the single or divorced mother, the widow, the foster mom, or the mother who may face the loss of a child. As I write, I pray for each parent who will read this book that though I can't speak to your specific situation in each entry, God will meet you where my words cannot.

Your Newborn Developmental Guide

Can you believe it? This little one you have longed for and cradled in your heart for nine long months is finally here. For most, this month will be full of firsts—first cuddles, first skin-to-skin contact, first feedings, first meetings with family, and more. Savor them. For those babies born prematurely, with health challenges, or to adoptive parents, your first few days or weeks may look different, but although the timelines and circumstances may vary, the firsts are just as precious.

Between the baby Apgar test; vitamin K shots; newborn screenings; and visits from nurses, lactation consultants, and family, your first few days will likely seem like a blur. The cocktail of interrupted sleep, discomfort, and anxiety, mixed with the joy of that squirming, downy-headed wonder is enough to leave any mother dizzy. Add in the hormone shifts your body is experiencing and the breast engorgement around day four to five, and no wonder the first week feels like a roller coaster ride. But take heart; soon enough your body and days will settle down again into a rhythm as comforting as that rocking chair in the nursery corner.

Your little one will likely sleep a lot, especially in the first days. Giving birth is exhausting; apparently, so is being born. Newborns need fourteen to seventeen hours of sleep per day and will typically wake to feed every two to four hours.

Don't be surprised if your little one loses weight in the first few days. This is normal. By week two, your baby will likely make his or her way back to their birthweight (usually ten to twelve days after birth). Breastfed babies should eat as much as they want at this stage, but a good rule of thumb for breastfed or formula-fed babies is sixteen to twenty-four ounces of breastmilk or formula in a twenty-four–hour period. Their stomachs are only the size of a walnut at this point, so it's no wonder they must eat often!

As the month goes on, expose Baby to natural light with open blinds and short walks (weather and your recovery permitting) in the daytime and keep lights low during night feedings; this will help Baby learn to distinguish night from day. And while interrupted sleep is, unfortunately, your current reality, try to grab some sleep when your baby sleeps. You need it; give yourself permission to take it.

Taking care of yourself is essential so you can take good care of your baby. Eat healthful, high-fiber foods as your body recovers from the stress of labor. Have some high-protein snacks available—like almonds, hard boiled eggs, or Greek yogurt—to provide you the energy to keep up with that little one. Use lanolin cream for sore nipples, and take a sitz bath to help soothe and heal the perineal area after labor. Graciously accept offers of delivered meals from friends or a relative's offer to hold the baby while you catch a quick nap or a take moment for yourself. As a reminder, these devotions and journaling spaces ahead are an invitation, not an obligation. Read what blesses you, write as you are able, and trust God at His Word that He gently leads those with young (Isaiah 40:11).

Our Good and Perfect Gift

Every good gift and every perfect gift
is from above, and comes down from
the Father of lights, with whom there is
no variation or shadow of turning.
JAMES 1:17

Oh the agony and ecstasy of Baby's arrival! No matter how your baby arrived—slow and deliberate, fast and furious, with an unexpected rush to the hospital or with a phone call from the adoption agency—your little one is here, and it's time to exhale. All those months of waiting are over, and whatever Baby's birth day held for you, now it's time to give thanks to God, the Giver of all good gifts, including this one so near to your beating heart.

It's easy to misunderstand gratitude in today's culture. Gratitude is more than just a feeling. Gratitude should be an action. We give thanks *to* the One who has given to us. The Bible is clear that every good and perfect gift is from above, from the Father of the heavenly lights. What a glorious reminder! The Creator of the stars that give light to everything we know is intimately involved in the creation of those tiny little fingers that now curl around your own.

Wherever you are right now, stop and take a few minutes not only to feel gratitude for your little one but to turn to God in prayer, thanking Him for all His mercies this day and in the months leading to this point.

The Ultimate Giver, the Ultimate Gift

*He who did not spare His own Son, but
delivered Him up for us all, how shall He
not with Him also freely give us all things?*

ROMANS 8:32

This week as you welcome your little one into the world, consider God as the ultimate Giver. God didn't hold anything back from us. He gave us His most precious and costly gift—His Son. Let this staggering truth take your breath away: Jesus, God's ultimate gift, died in our place that we might draw near to God. This is the generosity and love of our God. He gives freely. He loves freely. He lavishes us with His very best when we least deserve it. Let us never grow numb through familiarity.

Today as you hold your own precious son or daughter, let the weight of this verse sink deep into your heart. What great love the Father must have that He would give His precious Son for us. Paul, the author of Romans, asked rhetorically, If God did not hold back His Son, how will He not also freely give us all things?

If you are a believer, then as Romans 8:31 says, "God is for [you]." What are you anxious about this day, dear one? Transitioning home with Baby, nursing challenges, your own recovery—there is nothing too big or too small to bring to Him in prayer. Ask God and trust that He will give you all you need. How can He withhold what He deems best for you when He did not withhold His Son?

Treasuring Our Gifts

But Mary treasured up all these things
and pondered them in her heart.
LUKE 2:19 NIV

*Y*ou've been given a precious and astonishing gift this week. Truly, I believe every life is a miracle. What does God, the gift-giver, hope we will do with a gift given? Perhaps the simplest answer is this: treasure the gift. Deeply value, enjoy, and cherish it.

This is what we see Mary doing in today's verse. Certainly, she was treasuring the events surrounding Jesus' birth: the words spoken over Him, the significance of events, and the unfolding of God's providence in every detail of His arrival. But to say that she treasured these things and pondered them is also to say that she treasured Jesus and pondered Him. She oohed and aahed over Him, delighted in Him. The most perfect gift ever given was first treasured by a mother. Twice in Jesus' childhood, we read this sentiment. The second time is at the end of His childhood at age twelve (Luke 2:51). Jesus' childhood is bookended with His mother's treasuring.

Jesus flourished amid that treasuring love. He grew mentally, spiritually, physically, socially, and emotionally. "And Jesus grew in wisdom and stature, and in favor with God and man" (Luke 2:52 NIV). Treasuring a child prepares this rich soil, tilling the ground for the flowering of holistic growth. How amazing that we as mothers can be the first to treasure the gift of a human soul.

Take an inventory of wonders as you get to know the sweet bundle in your arms and praise God for it all, from that perfect dimple to those tiny feet. Describe your sweet little one—so new to you—and take a few minutes to thank God for this precious gift.

_____

_____

_____

_____

_____

_____

_____

What do you always want to remember about your little one's birth day?

_____

_____

_____

_____

_____

_____

_____

A Mother's Comfort

As one whom his mother comforts,
so I will comfort you; and you shall
be comforted in Jerusalem.
ISAIAH 66:13

𝒴ou know by now how quickly the sound of your baby's cry can bring you to your feet. An infant's cry cannot be ignored. Though the cry unnerves us, there is something equally amazing about being able to meet your child's needs. Often at this point, those cries simply mean your little one is hungry. Watching your baby relax in your arms as you nourish him or her by breast or bottle is awe-inspiring.

It makes sense that God would use this analogy of a mother and babe to help us understand how He comforts us. As stated a few verses earlier, "That you may nurse and be satisfied from her consoling breast; that you may drink deeply with delight from her glorious abundance" (Isaiah 66:11 ESV). When we feed on the nourishing Word of God in His loving embrace, our bodies and minds relax. Our God is abundant; His mercies, promises, and sovereign care satisfy us. And a satisfied soul is not easily perturbed. What a comfort to receive His love and acceptance as the determining voice of our worth! He longs to comfort us like a mother longs to comfort her child, if we but cry out to Him.

My Comfort in Anxiety

In the multitude of my anxieties within
me, Your comforts delight my soul.

PSALM 94:19

As new moms, we experience a host of anxieties. Let's face it, having a newborn is just a whole lot of new. All those shifting hormones in our bodies, lack of sleep, and amped-up emotions of joy and pain can intensify our already natural fears and doubts. But in the book of Philippians, Paul offered a solution: "Be anxious for nothing, but in everything by prayer and supplication, with thanksgiving, let your requests be made known to God" (4:6). When anxious thoughts enter our minds, we can turn each one into a prayer. In the next verse, Paul continued, "and the peace of God, which surpasses all understanding, will guard your hearts and minds through Christ Jesus" (4:7).

The psalmist certainly must have known something similar because he wrote, "In the multitude of my anxieties within me, Your comforts delight my soul" (94:19). Delight is about as opposite an emotion to anxiety as one can imagine. Delight evokes a face relaxed in joy rather than tensed in worry. The overwhelming peace of God standing guard over our hearts and minds is another striking image. Don't let anxiety overwhelm and shut you down. Take every anxious thought and transform it into a prayer. Let God comfort you, delight you, and guard you.

Comforted to Comfort

Praise be to the God and Father of our
Lord Jesus Christ, the Father of compassion
and the God of all comfort, who comforts
us in all our troubles, so that we can
comfort those in any trouble with the
comfort we ourselves receive from God.
2 CORINTHIANS 1:3–4 NIV

Friend, I know you are tired today. You've made it through another night of caring for a newborn. Your body is slowly healing, but you are still not 100 percent. You may be sore; you may wonder, *Can I do this?* Although I do not know the specifics of your situation, God does. He knows. He sees. He cares. Oh, the comfort of that thought! No hardship in your life is hidden from God. He not only cares intimately for you but also works on your behalf. Let the comfort of that thought sink in.

Once you experience that comfort for yourself, you will be able to offer comfort, whether that is soothing a crying baby or comforting a friend. But here's an interesting corollary: there are Christians in your circle who stand ready to comfort you too. They have received God's comfort—perhaps during a time like you are in—and may be waiting for the opportunity to bless you today. Accept the comfort available in His Word and from His people. Reach out if you are in need and give if you are full. This is our privilege and our calling.

Introducing your new one to others is one of the great joys of the first few weeks of your baby's life. Write about some precious introductions of Baby to friends and family.

This week, the verses in 2 Corinthians 1:3–4 remind us that to pass on the comfort we've received or the lessons we've learned is a blessing. What is a truth God has helped you understand that you look forward to sharing at the right time with your son or daughter?

God of Wonders

Many, O Lord my God, are Your
wonderful works which You have
done; and Your thoughts toward us
cannot be recounted to You in order.
PSALM 40:5

We live in an age of cynicism, where it's considered cool to be unimpressed. Because of that, even in these early days of motherhood, we can miss what's right before our eyes: the wonder. I don't say that to dismiss the hard things—they are real. But let's not miss this: a year ago this tiny human being didn't exist. Now a human soul nuzzles under your chin.

In the Old Testament, the word *wonder* occurs rarely. It is most often the translation of the word *mopheth*, meaning a splendid or conspicuous work—a miracle. Keep this in mind when the Bible calls God's works "wonderful." He is a God whose works are miraculous, marvelous, and awe-inspiring.

David certainly would have had in mind the wonders of the plagues that helped free the Israelites from Egypt, the parting of the Red Sea, God causing water to flow from a rock, His provision of manna in the wilderness, Jericho's walls crashing down, the taking of the promised land, and Goliath dead at his feet.

In today's psalm, God's works and thoughts are awe-inspiring. His wonderful thoughts toward us are too numerous to count. Blink and you'll miss that last part—His thoughts *toward* us. As you feel alone during the midnight feedings or anxious as you try to soothe Baby, His thoughts are toward you. This God who leaves miracles in His wake has put His thoughts on you. Meditate on that.

A Masterpiece

*I will praise You, for I am fearfully and
wonderfully made; marvelous are Your
works, and that my soul knows very well.*

PSALM 139:14

$\mathcal{A}$ s we learned in the last devotion, the word *wonder* is one not taken lightly in the Bible. We should read into that word all the awe and breathtaking splendor we possibly can. In today's verse, our wonderful God is seen at the apex of His marvel-making: creating you. Your heartbeat spontaneously burst to life around twenty days gestation. Every hair on your head, your eye color, and your personality are encoded in tiny strands of DNA. You grew from mere cells to the walking, talking miracle you are today. You are one of God's best wonders. His works— and, by extension, you and your baby—are marvelous.

Does your soul know this? Do you know that creation reached its crescendo when God created man and woman—in *His* likeness? Do you know that you and your little one are marvelous? I hope so. Because it changes us. God placed such value on you that He gave His very best—His Son—to bring you into His presence forever. He desires to be with you. He wants to be present with His people. Jesus, our Emmanuel, is God's ultimate sign of God's desire to be with us. Marvelous, isn't it?

May you see yourself and your baby with His eyes: you are His masterpiece!

Wonderful Counselor

For unto us a Child is born, unto us a Son is given; and the government will be upon His shoulder. And His name will be called Wonderful, Counselor, Mighty God, Everlasting Father, Prince of Peace.
ISAIAH 9:6

As you settle into new routines of life at home with Baby, you have focused this week on the truth that God is wonderful. You've learned that the Bible's interpretation of *wonderful* is not the *wonderful* your grade-school teacher scrawled on your book report. By *wonderful* the Bible means that God is a miracle-working, marvel-generating doer of conspicuously splendid deeds. You've studied that the apex of His creation was when He made us in His image. And you come now to the perfectly wonderful person of Christ. As fully God, He shows forth all God's wonder; as fully human, He is the perfect image-bearer.

His life is punctuated with wonders: the wonder of His birth, the miracles of His ministry, His resurrection, and His ascension. He is also wisdom incarnate. In Him "are hidden all the treasures of wisdom and knowledge" (Colossians 2:3). He is the "power of God and the wisdom of God" (1 Corinthians 1:24). As such, Jesus is our wonderful counselor, able to advise us with perfect wisdom and able to complete God's will with perfect power. What better counselor could you have during these challenging days with a newborn than one who has sympathized with our every weakness (Hebrews 4:15)? Doesn't that make you feel that you can exhale today as you rock that baby? Breathe, Mama; He's got you.

Calling to mind God's past wonderful works is a way to bolster faith in the present moment. Where have you seen God's marvels in your life so far? Meditate on these things and on His wonders recorded in the Word. These give us hope during the hard days.

Psalm 139:14 says that we are "fearfully and wonderfully made." How can you already see this to be true in your newborn?

The Prism of Perfect Joy

You will show me the path of life; in
Your presence is fullness of joy; at Your
right hand are pleasures forevermore.
PSALM 16:11

Imagine for a minute, before time, earth, sea, or sky, there was this: God as Trinity in perfect communion and perfect joy, in a constant, perfect fellowship in that triune harmony. And out of the overflowing joy of that relationship, God created sky and land and birds and fish and four-legged creatures and sunsets and moonlit nights and blooming flowers and fruits of every delicious kind. And ultimately, that joy bubbled over in the creation of man and woman. You are an overflow of God's perfect joy.

To be in the presence of God is to be in the reflecting prism of joy, bouncing perfectly off Father, Son, and Holy Spirit—the fullness of joy. Tired and weary as you are, dear mother friend, you have been invited into the epicenter of joy itself. Whatever stress and weariness you are facing right now, close your eyes for just a moment and enter into this joyful fellowship with Him. Ask God to give you a taste of His joy in the perfect fellowship of the Trinity. Ask Him to fill you with the joy of His presence even on this ordinary day in the life of mothering your precious new baby.

Catching Joy

These things I have spoken to you,
that My joy may remain in you,
and that your joy may be full.
JOHN 15:11

Four short weeks ago, you held your beautiful baby in your arms for the first time. The joy of those first few days with a newborn is hard to match. But as the burdens of the twenty-four-hour care begin to weigh on you, the euphoria subsides. While not all our moments will be happy ones, God does want joy to be our constant companion. (Note well: happiness depends on circumstance; joy does not.) Joy is one of God's attributes that He wants us to catch, what theologians call "communicable." Incommunicable attributes, such as God's omnipotence, omnipresence, and omniscience, are attributes of His you will not receive, regardless of how long you're in eternity with Him.

But how exactly do you catch joy? In today's passage, Jesus explained our relationship to Him in terms of the vine and branches; we are connected to Him in a life-sustaining way. Without Him, we cannot bear fruit. But if we cultivate a habit of closeness, keeping His commands, we will abide in His love. Have you ever spent time with someone who is so joyful that in their presence you find yourself perking up? God is the burning center of joy. If we cultivate a habit of closeness, His joy will remain in us. It can be as simple as taking a moment while feeding Baby to say, "Oh God, keep me close to You, and let Your joy overflow in me." There is no quick fix for joy; it's a daily habit of cultivating closeness. But oh, mamas, His joy is available! And it is a gift we so desperately need!

For the Joy Set Before You

*Let us run with endurance the race that is
set before us, looking unto Jesus, the author
and finisher of our faith, who for the joy
that was set before Him endured the cross.*
HEBREWS 12:1–2

$\mathcal{M}$ otherhood is not a sprint. It is a pure endurance run. Whether this is your first leg or mile thirteen, it will take grit and determination. But we also need to keep our eyes on the prize. Jesus is our ultimate example. He endured the worst hardship imaginable: the pain, rejection, and separation from God on the cross. He took on the full weight of sin for us. And He did it for the joy set before Him, glorifying the Father and bringing many sons and daughters into glory.

We have a chance to imitate Jesus daily in our motherhood. For the joy set before us, we endure sleep-interrupted nights, mastitis, even diaper blowouts. We endure sacrifices—days of frustration, disappointment, drudgery, and thanklessness. If we are doing it for the wrong reasons, we will burn out. We don't do it for our fulfillment, for the joy our kids bring, or to fill our loneliness. We mother for the glory of God. We nourish life as a living act of worship. With this orientation, our most menial acts transform into service to the King! Soak this in. Let the joy set before you give you endurance for each mile.

What moments or little milestones have brought you joy in the last few weeks with your little one? Have you given Baby a first bath or held him while he slept nuzzled on your chest? Record one of these sweet joys here.

_____

_____

_____

_____

_____

_____

_____

Read Matthew 25:21. How would you describe "the joy of your Lord"? How can this future hope impact you today?

_____

_____

_____

_____

_____

_____

_____

Monthly Memories and Milestones

Our baby's full name: _____

How we chose that name: _____

_____

_____

_____

Baby's Birthdate

Date: _____

Time: _____

Place: _____

Newborn Stats

Length: _____

Weight: _____

Eye Color: _____

Hair Color: _____

Labor and Delivery

It all started when . . .

I knew I was in labor when . . .

I was really nervous about . . .

I was really excited about . . .

The special people in the room were . . .

Your One-Month-Old Developmental Guide

You are one month in love with this sweet little boy or girl. This month you can expect something you've been waiting for: the dawning of your baby's first social smiles, which usually happens around the six-week mark. When your baby gives that first social smile, you will know it. It will include eye contact and facial expression in addition to lips. It will be a smile in response to you. If you don't see this develop this month, mention it to your pediatrician.

What else can you look forward to this month? Your baby may be growing out of those newborn clothes! Most infants will gain weight and grow between 1 to 1$\frac{1}{2}$ inches in height by the end of the month.

Your little one's eyes will begin to track objects this month. You may find her eyes follow you when you come into the room and will follow a toy moved in front of her face from side to side. By month's end, Baby may reach for those objects and possibly swat at them, a sign of emerging hand-eye coordination and depth perception.

Speaking of what is holding your little one's attention these days: contrasting colors, lines, and checkerboard patterns are especially fascinating. Your baby is taking in information about the world through all his senses, so soft baby toys with different textures are a great way for Baby to learn about the world.

Aside from stimulating your child's senses, you can also help Baby develop muscle strength. Increasing tummy time in small increments helps build core strength. If your baby hates tummy time (like mine always have), the best thing to do is to get down on the floor with them. Let them see you smiling and encouraging them at their eye level.

Some babies (about 15 percent) may develop colic around this time. If Baby cries more than three hours daily, and hunger or sleep is not the cause, talk to your pediatrician.

Whether your baby is experiencing colic or just normal fussiness, know your limits. It is okay to put Baby down in a safe place and walk away for a few minutes to regain your calm. If you ever feel like shaking the baby, definitely put him or her down and call your spouse, a friend, or a neighbor. These can be overwhelming times.

If you are feeling overwhelmed, know you aren't alone. About 80 percent of moms experience the baby blues in the month after baby is born, with 20 percent experiencing severe postpartum depression or anxiety disorder, which can happen anytime during the first year. This is marked by lack of or excess appetite, loss of interest in activities, severe mood swings, inability to concentrate, excessive crying, heightened anxiety or panic attacks, obsessive thoughts, or inability to care for oneself or the baby. If you think you are suffering from postpartum depression or anxiety, contact your doctor. This is a serious issue.

But back to that fabulous little one whose sleeping patterns are holding steady at fourteen to seventeen hours a day. For some blessed mamas, longer nighttime stretches may start developing at six weeks past baby's due date. Four or five daytime naps are still quite normal, as well as about eight feedings a day for breastfed babies, and about sixteen to twenty-four ounces of breastmilk or formula for a twenty-four-hour period.

Soul Rest

Come to Me, all you who labor and are heavy laden, and I will give you rest. Take My yoke upon you and learn from Me, for I am gentle and lowly in heart, and you will find rest for your souls. For My yoke is easy and My burden is light.

MATTHEW 11:28–30

Is it cruel to include a devotional week on rest for mamas who are sleep-deprived? Trust me, I thought about it. And my conclusion is, no. Rest is more than just sleep, although that is important too. Resting in Jesus is ceasing to strive. We trust in Him and not our good works to give us salvation. Resting in Jesus is giving Him our anxious thoughts. God is our rest because He is our provider. He knows our needs. He will not abandon us. Resting in Jesus is turning over burdens He doesn't want us to carry. What burdens have you chosen? Is your burden a perfectly tidy home, a weight goal, a level of material comfort? Come to Him and take His yoke—His yoke is easy; our yokes are not.

God may not be asking you to do anything for Him right now except care for yourself and your baby. Your worth is not in your doing. It is in Him. Rest is available to us even on the days we are sleep-deprived. It is a rest rooted in His nature: He is gentle and humble. We are often harsher taskmasters than gentle Jesus. Dear one, come to Him and let Him untie the unnecessary loads. See where He wants to give your soul rest.

A Rest That Re-creates Me

*Remember the Sabbath day, to keep it
holy. Six days you shall labor and do
all your work, but the seventh day is
the Sabbath of the LORD your God.*
EXODUS 20:8–10

R est? Is she kidding? I'd love to rest, but that's not happening with a one-month-old! If you are thinking rest is impossible with a young one, I want to encourage you to ask God to show you the way. He wants your soul to rest, even amid nights of interrupted sleep. Sabbath reminds us to stop and let God care for us. It reminds us that caring for our souls is deeply important. It is a priority that re-creates us on a weekly basis.

Sabbath points us to God as our ultimate rest. When we take a day away from work, we trust He is our true provider and that every good thing is from Him. When we take a day to rest, we invite God to reinvigorate us for our work.

How can you find Sabbath rest amid life with a one-month-old? There isn't a formula. But begin with your heart. Take your Sabbath day and set it apart. Use it to honor God as the center of your life. Do what you can to make this day easy and delightful to your soul. Rearrange your week to help make this the day you anticipate and savor most. As we do this, we find God weeds out the wrong priorities, the unnecessary burdens. We lean into the habits of rest and trust. We discover our souls cared for in ways that re-energize us to work vigorously for Him on the other six days.

Sail Away with Me

*So they went away by themselves
in a boat to a solitary place.*
MARK 6:32 NIV

The year my oldest son turned seven, I had children ages five, three, one, and newborn. Some days I wondered if I'd ever survive. Life with that many little people is one of constant pulling: pulling for needs, for attention, for a little piece of you. When I read in the Gospels of Jesus' ministry, I feel a kinship with Him as the crowds seemed to almost smother Him, clamoring for a miracle, a touch, a word, just nearness. He could have healed twenty-four hours a day, seven days a week. He was fully God after all. But He did not. He knew His earthly ministry was brief—just three years! And yet He is shown in the Gospels as deliberately drawing away from the crowds to pray, to share close moments with His twelve disciples, and to sleep.

Sweet mama friend, let me whisper a secret to you: you are not superwoman. You cannot do it all and not rest. I think as mamas sometimes we expect ourselves to be superhuman, but God reminds us that we are not. In the end, remembering we need rest is remembering we need grace. It is remembering we are not God. And it is remembering we need the intimacy of time with Him and with our soul-friends to be able to do all that He asks. Will you come away with Him?

What Sabbath day habits can you develop that will eventually make life sweeter for your little one?

Speaking of rest, how does your baby like to sleep these days? In your arms, swaddled, in the car, in a baby carrier? Describe it here.

A Grace We So Desperately Need

And the LORD passed before him and proclaimed, "The LORD, the LORD God, merciful and gracious, longsuffering, and abounding in goodness and truth."
EXODUS 34:6

As we consider our gracious God this week, it's natural that we start in this verse, where the word *gracious* is introduced. Remember the context: God has delivered His people from slavery, brought them through the Red Sea, covenanted with them, and given them the Ten Commandments. But while Moses was still on Mount Sinai, the people of Israel built an idol and worshiped it. Unbelievable, right? The Lord was rightfully enraged. But Moses interceded, and God chose to show His unmerited favor. As He did with the Israelites, our gracious God gives us favor when we do not deserve it. He treats us as His treasured possession when we act nothing like it.

Mamas, where do you need grace today? Have your hormones felt like a roller coaster that has you strapped in for a wild ride? Have you snapped at the people who love you because you are coasting on coffee? Here's the deal: we worship a God of grace! That doesn't give us license to sin. It does give us enormous comfort as we strive to be like Him and fail, repeatedly. I don't know where you need grace today, but I know it is available to you. I know God loves you and is cheering you on, but He also stands ready to catch you when you fall. That's who He is; our God is gracious. Hold fast to this truth.

A Gracious Longing

Yet the LORD longs to be gracious to you;
therefore he will rise up to show you
compassion. For the LORD is a God of
justice. Blessed are all who wait for him!
ISAIAH 30:18 NIV

When you look on your little one, doesn't your heart fill with longings for him—for joy, for growth, for a relationship one day with Jesus? You look on that baby and yearn for every good thing possible for him. Now fast-forward. Your little one is a child. He has just betrayed your trust, lied, disappointed you. You must deal with the sin. That is clear. But has your longing for good things for this child changed? In fact, even as you discipline, you long for the consequences to right your child's heart.

Just before today's verse, Isaiah vividly described how Israel had rebelled against God: "Ah, stubborn children," he called them, "lying children, children unwilling to hear the instruction of the LORD" (30:1, 9 ESV). God's children have sinned repeatedly, but God's posture toward them hasn't changed. He "longs to be gracious." When we sin, our tendency is to run and hide. But if we could picture God as longing to be gracious, surveying the horizon like the Prodigal's father, yearning for our homecoming, it would change us. He actively longs to redeem and restore. He rises with eager willingness to do good toward us. Let that grace change us today.

A Gracious Gift

*For it is by grace you have been saved,
through faith—and this is not from
yourselves, it is the gift of God—not
by works, so that no one can boast.*
EPHESIANS 2:8–10 NIV

What does God want to teach us through the exhaustion of these early days with a new baby? Perhaps a lesson about grace. Sometimes when we are exhausted, we just can't. We can't take the meal to the family in need. We can't sign up for the ministry that could desperately use an extra hand. We can't because we don't have anything else to give. And you know what? That's okay. (*Gasp!*)

Yes, it's okay. It's okay because God doesn't love you for what you do for Him. He loves you simply because He is love. It's okay because the success of God's great plans don't rest on your shoulders, but on His. It's okay because life has seasons, and you are in an especially demanding one.

When I was younger, I read the biography of Amy Carmichael, a famous missionary to India who cared for hundreds of orphaned children. The thing that impressed me most was what she learned at the end of her life. After a lifetime of *doing* for Jesus, she was stuck in bed. While her mind was strong, her body was not. And for the first time, she learned that God did not love her for what she *did* for Him—but that He simply loved her. While God certainly is pleased when we join Him in serving others, He does not *need* us. He loves us even when all we can do is lie in bed. He loves us because He is gracious.

What comfort does it give you knowing that you don't have to perform to earn God's love?

Your life with Baby is composed of many ordinary moments that when strung together make an extraordinary garland of love. What ordinary moments with your little one do you want to remember from this week?

The Thundering Strength of God

*The voice of the LORD is over the
waters; the God of glory thunders.*
PSALM 29:3

I spent most of my childhood living within miles of the beach, and as far back as I can remember, I have loved to watch a thunderstorm move in over the ocean. Sometimes within a matter of minutes, sparkling waters morph to reflect the ominous hues of the approaching dark clouds. Lightning splits the sky, while the waves claw and pummel the shoreline in endless competition. Rain turns the ocean into its kettle drum, and thunder builds to a crescendo. There is raw, unfiltered power in a storm.

Psalm 29 is the storm-lover's psalm. Commentators conjecture that David wrote this psalm after watching a storm move eastward over the Mediterranean. It is a hymn to the God of strength, the one who "breaks the cedars," who "twists the oaks," and "strips the forests bare" (Psalm 29:5, 9 NIV). In this psalm we get a close-up picture of the mighty strength of God, who snaps cedars like toothpicks, who has the power to unleash the fury of storm or flood, but who exercises even greater strength in His self-control. Our God wields His strength for the good of His people. Mamas, that strength is for you today amid eyes that can't stay open, arms tired of holding, a mind fatigued with care—the strength of a hero for you. Read this psalm and let the echo of His strength roll over you like the storm-churned waves. If you feel weak or tired or worn down today, remember: this strong God exercises His strength for His glory and your good.

A Holy Fearlessness

The LORD is my light and my salvation; whom shall I fear? The LORD is the strength of my life; of whom shall I be afraid?

PSALM 27:1

For many new moms, with Baby's birth comes a new host of anxieties. Some of those fears are unfounded or at least unlikely to happen. Others are rooted in very real, daily concerns. But God does not want us to live under the crushing weight of anxiety. He wants us to know His strength, to be comforted by the steadfast assurance of His goodness in mediating that strength.

In today's psalm, we see David's holy fearlessness. With God as his light and salvation, whom does he need to fear? Light points to God's ability to illuminate our present darkness. Salvation points to the assurance of our future rescue (even if we are not rescued from our current situation). We hear in this psalm a foreshadowing of Paul's famous words in Romans 8:31: "If God is for us, who can be against us?"

We can join both David and Paul in this holy fearlessness if we understand the strength and goodness of our God. While He may not intercede in our current situation in the way we hope or even expect, we can be sure that He who did not spare His Son for us is not going to let us down (Romans 8:32). He has a plan; we don't need to be anxious. He has bought for us a future; we need not fear today or tomorrow.

His Strength in Our Weakness

And He said to me, "My grace is sufficient
for you, for My strength is made perfect
in weakness." Therefore most gladly I
will rather boast in my infirmities, that
the power of Christ may rest upon me.
2 CORINTHIANS 12:9

The months immediately following childbirth can make us feel at our weakest. Let's face it: our bodies have been stretched and rearranged, only to climax in a painful eviction of our nine-month tenant. As we recover, we may be healing from physical wounds while giving sustenance round-the-clock. We are tired, drained, and—because of hormones— more emotional than normal. If there is a time in our lives when the word *weakness* might be rightfully applied, it is this time.

But today's passage about weakness, in our worldly way of thinking, surprises us. Here's what it doesn't say: "God shakes His head at your weakness." It doesn't say, "God wishes you'd pull yourself together and get a grip." Nope. Not even close. The passage says God delights in making His strength known in our weakness. In fact, in some mysterious way, His strength is made perfect in weakness.

So if you are feeling down because you can hardly find the time for a shower or barely form a complete thought, remember that God doesn't look at your weakness as a liability. He sees it as an opportunity for demonstrating the enormity of His power. His strength is made perfect in our weakness.

What strong people in your personal life do you want your baby to know about one day? Is there a grandparent or a mentor who epitomized strength exercised with goodness? Did that strength give you a feeling of safety and security?

Babies, just like us, can become anxious. Do you have any favorite lullabies, songs, or hymns you like to sing to calm or soothe Baby?

Under His Wings of Refuge

The LORD repay your work, and
a full reward be given you by the
LORD God of Israel, under whose
wings you have come for refuge.
RUTH 2:12

oes it ever feel like your good work isn't noticed? All of us mamas have felt that invisibility amid changing diapers and waking up through the night. One of the things the book of Ruth shows us, however, is that God sees our quiet sacrifice.

Though she was free of obligation when her husband died, Ruth decided to journey back to Israel with her mother-in-law, Naomi, to support her by gleaning among the leftover sheaves day after day. And in today's verse, Boaz, the owner of the field where Ruth gleaned, said to Ruth that he hoped the God in whom she took refuge would reward her. Ironically, God was already at work through Boaz. God—the ultimate wing of refuge for Ruth and Naomi—used Boaz to be His earthly protector of these widows, first when Boaz let Ruth glean in his field and then when he married her.

In the book of Matthew, Jesus reiterated that He sees our quiet work. He reminded us, "Whatever you did for one of the least of these . . . you did for me" (25:40 NIV). Surely caring for a tiny infant who cannot even say thank you qualifies. This verse reminds us that all our work can be done unto the Lord as a spiritual act of worship. And these acts do not go unnoticed—they will receive an inheritance from the Lord.

The Refuge of Generations

How priceless is your unfailing
love, O God! People take refuge
in the shadow of your wings.
PSALM 36:7 NIV

I love the image in the Bible of the wings of refuge. It's only used a handful of times (from Boaz to Ruth in Ruth 2:12 and in a few of David's psalms: 17:8; 36:7; 57:1; 61:4; 63:7; and 91:4). When I think of this peculiarly beautiful image, I have to wonder: Did Boaz or Ruth tell their great story of God's wings of refuge to their son Obed? Did Obed pass it on to his son Jesse? Did David hear often at Jesse's knee of how God spread His wings of refuge over his great-grandmother Ruth? Did these words fill that shepherd boy's imaginations on the long nights in the field and comfort him when he fled from Saul? Perhaps that story told and retold might be why the image made it into David's songs. I wouldn't be surprised: our words matter.

The words and stories we pass down to our children impact them. We are instructed to teach our children about God when we sit, when we walk, when we lie down, and when we rise (Deuteronomy 6:6–7). We are instructed to tell about what God has done (Psalm 78:4–6) so that the next generation will know. We can take refuge in the shadow of His wings because the ones who went before us found Him a faithful refuge. What stories of God's faithfulness will you pass on to your child one day?

A Very Present Help

God is our refuge and strength, a
very present help in trouble.
PSALM 46:1

$\mathcal{N}$othing epitomizes strength like a fortress. Psalm 46 depicts an impressive bulwark of protection—a refuge where we can hide and not be afraid "though the earth gives way, though the mountains be moved into the heart of the sea, though its waters roar and foam, though the mountains tremble" (Psalm 46:2–3 ESV). A "very present help" aptly describes this fortification and is the image God wants to invoke to remind us that He is so near to us, so powerfully surrounding us, so utterly *for* us. God is our insurmountable, unshakable, impenetrable refuge.

In the New Testament, God gives us an even more tangible image of "a very present help." It is Jesus, whose very name means "God with us." Life with a new baby can be such an isolating time—how beautiful it is to remember that God is present with us, even when we feel so alone. When Jesus left earth, He comforted His disciples with these words: "And I will pray the Father, and He will give you another Helper, that He may abide with you forever—the Spirit of truth. . . . You know him, for He dwells with you and will be in you. I will not leave you orphans" (John 14:16–18). God, our refuge, surrounding us; Christ, our Emmanuel, beside us; and the Spirit, our advocate, within us: surely, we do not lack for help. Loneliness as mothers is real, but His presence is a sure and present comfort.

The softness of the image of wings of refuge reminds me of the softness of a mother's arms or a cozy receiving blanket. Where does your baby seem most comfortable and relaxed? What is soothing him or her these days?

A refuge can also be a place of retreat where we find God. Has there been a particular place that has been meaningful to you that you would like to tell your future grown son or daughter about one day?

Monthly Memories
and Milestones

During Baby's first eight weeks, our little one met some special
people, including . . .

_____

_____

_____

_____

The first time we took Baby somewhere was to go to . . .

_____

_____

_____

_____

My favorite thing to dress Baby in is . . .

_____

_____

_____

_____

One adjustment we've had to make since Baby arrived was . . .

Other moments or milestones from this month:

Your Two-Month-Old Developmental Guide

Well, that went by fast, didn't it? Your baby is already two months old! Look how he is changing: he has more control over his body and can hold his head up for brief periods during tummy time. He concentrates on your face and may show signs of recognizing you. He may be smiling or vocalizing with coos and raspberries.

But your baby is not the only one changing. You are learning to differentiate your baby's cries, learning what positions and techniques soothe your baby, and perhaps mastering the power nap. If so, good for you! If not, there's a light at the end of the tunnel, as most babies begin sleeping longer stretches by twelve weeks. You may also be making choices about going back to work or staying home full-time. Make these decisions prayerfully, knowing whatever God shows you, He will provide all your needs: He will be your strength as you seek Him.

This month your baby will continue needing between fourteen to seventeen hours of sleep. Some babies will begin taking less-frequent naps, but napping for longer durations.

Your little one will also continue to need to eat about six to eight times per day. He will give you cues that he's hungry by making sucking noises, putting hands toward his mouth, and whimpering. Baby's growth spurts vary, so continue to be sensitive to his cues. Don't compare him with other babies; instead, look to his individual growth chart the pediatrician is tracking. This is the time many babies start getting chunky. Enjoy those dimpled thighs and chubby cheeks if your baby has them; crawling, walking, and running will melt away those lovable baby rolls soon enough.

Speaking of feeding, you've become an expert by now, no doubt, in changing those dirty diapers. If you are noticing fewer than six to eight wet diapers a day, your baby might be dehydrated. Your baby's soiled diapers will be less predictable. Some babies may have poopy diapers several times a day, while others may have them once a week.

You may also notice your baby's vision improving. Around this time your baby can see objects clearly about a foot away. And you will notice distance vision improving soon when she turns her face to follow your movements around the room. Color perception is also growing this month as well as fascination with circle patterns and spirals. Your face and other familiar faces are still the main attraction, though. Make sure to give your baby plenty of facial responses. Resist the temptation to look at your phone instead of Baby. You will find your baby likes to mirror your face and emotions. Make the most of this by giving her plenty of expressions to mimic. This mirroring play is a great first game and stimulates neural functions involved in social interactions later in life.

Thrice Holy

And one cried to another and said:
"Holy, holy, holy is the LORD of hosts;
the whole earth is full of His glory!"
ISAIAH 6:3

*T*here is something about a baby that is so pure: tiny feet without calluses, soft skin without wrinkles, lips without unkind words. But while our babies are untainted by time, only God is untainted by moral failure. Only God is perfectly holy. Of all the attributes, this is the only one repeated in a threefold pattern, symbolic to the Israelites as the number of perfection and completion.

Though God calls us to be holy, He is alone in the supremacy of His holiness. Hannah, a mother like you, took time out to reflect on God's goodness to her in giving her a baby. She worshiped God in His holiness, declaring, "No one is holy like the LORD, for there is none besides You" (1 Samuel 2:2). No human can match God in holiness. Because of God's holiness, He cannot tolerate sin—even so-called small sin—in His presence. This is why we need a Savior. We long to be with God and yet cannot approach Him. In fact, in this passage when Isaiah looked on the Lord, his first response was, "Woe is me, for I am undone!" (Isaiah 6:5). There is really only one fitting reaction to such a thrice-holy God. The angels naturally do it, and the elders described in Revelation do it. They worship. They cast their crowns at His feet and declare that He is worthy of all glory, honor, and power (Revelation 4:11). And like Hannah, we, too, can pause in the midst of motherhood and worship God in His holiness.

Set Apart

But you are a chosen generation, a royal
priesthood, a holy nation, His own
special people, that you may proclaim
the praises of Him who called you out
of darkness into His marvelous light.

1 PETER 2:9

Unfortunately, the word *holy* has become dusty and antiquated. Sometimes, as Christians we don't know what to do with the word. The Bible calls us to be holy, but what does that mean?

The Bible defines holiness as something set apart, like a holy vessel, consecrated for special purposes. To be holy is to be distinct from all that is ordinary. And when it describes a holy people, it is referring to a people set apart by living in a radically different way.

Moms, as Christ-followers you have been set apart to live in a radically different way. If I could zoom in on one particular way right now, it is that you have been given the high and holy calling to motherhood. This passage calls you a part of "a royal priesthood" whose purpose is to proclaim His praise. As a mother, you are called to proclaim His praise to this babe all the days of his life. Your child, this infant before you, is a soul—of inexpressible worth to God. You are a steward of this precious gift. Jesus—our ultimate example of holiness, of a radically set-apart life—shows us the way forward. Leading by serving, rising by dying to self, we proclaim God through word and deed. Don't ever buy into the belief that mothering is unimportant work. It is holy work.

A Holy Prayer

And may the Lord make you increase and abound in love to one another and to all, just as we do to you, so that He may establish your hearts blameless in holiness.
1 THESSALONIANS 3:12–13

How does the Bible explain holiness? In this letter from Paul to the Thessalonians, he prayed earnestly that God might make these believers "increase and abound in love" not just to each other but to all people. He prayed this so God might establish their hearts "in holiness."

A big part of holiness is abounding in love. This makes sense because we know that "God is love" (1 John 4:8). If God is love, and God is completely holy, then it follows that love is a big part of what it means to be holy. But how do we grow in this kind of love today, right where we are? You can start by praying for love to abound through you to your infant. That love might look simple. Perhaps it is the gift of your attention. Give this tiny one the gift of your eyes. Look at him. Talk to him. Notice the wonders of how God has made him. And give this baby the gift of your delight. Enjoy this little one. Smile at him. Laugh with him. Enjoy the mirroring affection of communicating through babbles, coos, and smiles your pure delight in him. God's love flows into your baby through such ordinary, yet extraordinary, moments. Let these simple acts re-teach you how to love all people: by giving them the gifts of your attention and delight in who God has made them to be.

Read Revelation 4:11. Isaiah's response to God's holiness was to offer himself in service to God, saying, "Here am I! Send me." (6:8). How is the Spirit calling you today to respond to the holy, holy, holy God?

Write a prayer that your little one might be set apart to the Lord. Ask that he would grow in holiness and pattern his life after Jesus.

Merciful: The God We Need

"I will make all my goodness pass before you and will proclaim before you my name 'The Lord.' And I will be gracious to whom I will be gracious, and will show mercy on whom I will show mercy."
EXODUS 33:19 ESV

When we feel like a hot mess, bawling for no reason, struggling to get a crying baby strapped into a car seat, or snapping at the slow cashier because Baby is about to melt down, we might mistakenly think that God in His perfection couldn't possibly understand us in our struggle. Oh sweet mama friends, in these challenging days how acutely we feel the need for a merciful God! One who has pity on us and can consider all our weaknesses and sinful tendencies. We need One who forebears, One who shows compassion, and One who is gentle in all His ways. But good news! This God we need is the God we have!

In today's passage in Exodus, when God was making Himself known to Moses, He chose to make His goodness pass before Him. And that goodness was embodied in two words: *grace* and *mercy*. Grace is giving us what we do not deserve. In a sense, mercy is the other side of this coin: it is *not* giving us what we *do* deserve. When you think of all the things God could have chosen to reveal to Moses about His nature, isn't it telling that He chose to reveal what is most essential for Moses (and for us) to know Him: His grace and mercy. Yes, God is holy. Yes, God requires perfect obedience. But in His mercy He sent Jesus to be the answer to our imperfection.

Confident in His Mercy

Let us then approach God's throne of grace with confidence, so that we may receive mercy and find grace to help us in our time of need.

HEBREWS 4:16 NIV

After each of my babies arrived, there was a flurry of help: a stay from my parents, meals from the church, and once, parental leave for my husband. But each time there was a point where the extra help stopped, and boy, did I still need it. I might even say I needed it more. That little newborn was a bit older and not sleeping quite so easily, and I hadn't adjusted to the new normal. Maybe you haven't had any help at all, or maybe like me you've come to the end of the freezer meals. Either way, it can leave us feeling frazzled and, frankly, desperate.

The book of Hebrews focuses on how Jesus is the perfect priest. As a priest, He represents the people to God. As a perfect priest, He fully identifies with us, but He also fully takes our place. The author of Hebrews wrote, "For we do not have a high priest who is unable to empathize with our weaknesses, but we have one who has been tempted in every way, just as we are—yet he did not sin" (4:15 NIV). So Christ is able to fully sympathize with us and fully pay our price. This is His mercy. And it gives us confidence to draw near—near to the One who sympathizes with us, near to the One who has taken our penalty. This gives us confidence to ask boldly for our needs because His help never dries up.

Kyrie Eleison

Have mercy on me!
MATTHEW 15:22

*I*n these early days with Baby, we mothers don't have much time or energy. The times I've lacked brain power—because kids take it out of us—I've been grateful for the little prayers from the Bible that spring to mind. And I find my breath punctuated by these little prayers as reflexes throughout the day as I need His grace. These are prayers inspired by spiritual ancestors such as David, "Create in me a clean heart" (Psalm 51:10); or an unnamed father, "I believe; help my unbelief" (Mark 9:24).

But of all the little prayers I find myself praying, most often it is this one: "Have mercy on me." Not surprisingly, it is the most frequent request made of Jesus in the Gospels. Jesus heard this plea from blind men, a Canaanite woman whose daughter was oppressed by demons, a father whose son was plagued by epilepsy, Bartimaeus, a rich man, ten lepers, a tax collector, and beggars (see Matthew 9:27; 15:22; 17:15; 20:30–31; Mark 10:47–48; Luke 16:24; 17:13; 18:13, 38–39). These words have echoed throughout the history of the early Christian church, handed down in liturgy after liturgy in this two-word Greek phrase, *Kyrie eleison*, meaning "Lord, have mercy." While it is one of the simplest prayers, it is also one of the most profound. When we can't put our needs into words, "Have mercy on me" is the soul's way of saying "please," and God loves to answer.

Some people use simple prayers like "Have mercy on me!" to help them calm their minds. They breathe in while saying, "Lord, Jesus Christ, my Savior," and breathe out while saying, "Have mercy on me a sinner." Many of the Bible's prayers could be broken up in this way. Take a few minutes to write down some of these breath prayers, using your favorite scriptures. If you need a little help, look up passages like Psalm 46:10, Psalm 23, and Romans 8:38–39.

Write a prayer for your child to one day understand the mercy of God and to be merciful like our Father in heaven.

God's Covenant Faithfulness

The steadfast love of the LORD never ceases; his mercies . . . are new every morning; great is your faithfulness.
LAMENTATIONS 3:22–23 ESV

As parents, we know that nothing is more important to give to our children than steadfast love. Our kids need a love they can count on whether they are being nice or naughty, on their good days and bad. We know that for our children to blossom they need such faithful love.

In Hebrew there is an important word that is often translated as "steadfast love." It is *hesed*, and in the original language it implies a covenantal faithfulness. In the ancient Near East, people took covenants very seriously; they were often made to offer protection to weaker nations in exchange for service. Remember the covenant ceremony described in Genesis 15:1–15 between God and Abraham? In one of the great reversals, the smoldering firepot (representing God) moved through the sacrifices. It should have been Abraham, the weaker party, making the promise. Instead, God said that if He failed to keep His covenant with His people, let Him be torn asunder.

In Lamentations 3, this is that same kind of steadfast love, or *hesed*. God's covenant faithfulness never ceases; it never dries up; it never runs out. It is new every morning. Though we may fail, He will not fail. Though our emotions about God may shift, though our faithfulness will falter, though we have doubts or fears, God's steadfast love will not change. It is a searchlight beckoning us not to give up hope but instead to draw near.

Never-Ending Psalm

Give thanks to the LORD, for he is good,
for his steadfast love endures forever.

PSALM 136:1 ESV

$\mathcal{S}$ ome of the most famous lullabies are ones that could be sung on an infinite loop. They are comforting, repetitive, and rhythmical. Psalm 136 shares this self-soothing quality. Of its twenty-six verses, all end with "for his steadfast love endures forever." Psalm 136 is likely a very ancient psalm, where one of the Levites would call out a reason for thankfulness and the congregation would respond in unison with the refrain. Its five movements detail His steadfast love in different points in history: before creation (vv. 1–4), in creation (vv. 5–9), in deliverance from Egypt (vv. 10 15), in the wilderness and entering the promised land (vv. 16–22), and in His ongoing deliverance and help (vv. 23 26).

This repetition and movement through time represents God's unending, steadfast love. How it endured when His hand was clearly with them and when they wondered where He was. It was a way for God's people to rehearse His faithfulness, fulfilling the call in Deuteronomy 6:7 to pass these truths on to the next generation. As the psalm ends, there is an implicit invitation to continue adding to it with our fresh experiences of God's steadfast love. I wonder if we will hear many new verses to this song in eternity. But for now, let the refrain bounce and echo off the walls of your heart.

A Steadfast Anchor

This hope we have as an anchor of the
soul, both sure and steadfast, and which
enters the Presence behind the veil.
HEBREWS 6:19

*Y*our little one is constantly growing. Just when you perfect the art of swaddling, he gets a little stronger and breaks free, waking himself up again. Just when you finally figure out how to carry Baby in that cloth sling someone gave you for your baby shower, he gets too heavy for it, and you need something more supportive. Figuring out motherhood is like trying to jump aboard a moving train. We are always one step behind. How good, then, it is to know that in this ever-changing world with our growing babies, something remains constant.

Here in Hebrews, that constant is the ascended and resurrected Jesus, our certain promise of God's covenant faithfulness. This anchor is a sure catch in a world adrift. This anchor will hold. And I know that this promise is true because as the author of Hebrews says in the preceding verses, when God "wanted to make the unchanging nature of his purpose very clear to the heirs of what was promised, he confirmed it with an oath. God did this so that, by two unchangeable things in which it is impossible for God to lie, we who have fled to take hold of the hope set before us may be greatly encouraged" (6:17–18 NIV). Jesus, our steadfast hope in an uncertain world, enters behind the veil. He becomes the anchor of our souls, the promise that God will not forget us.

Your baby needs to know that while you will need to have rules and discipline as she grows, your love is steadfast and unconditional. Write a prayer for God's strength to help you remain steadfast in your love.

What lullabies do you like to sing to your little one? Or can you remember any special songs often sung to you or your siblings when you were younger?

Slow to Anger

Yet he was merciful; he forgave their
iniquities and did not destroy them.
Time after time he restrained his anger
and did not stir up his full wrath.
PSALM 78:38 NIV

Mothering in these early months requires so much patience: patience with the baby who wakes up the moment you put her down, patience with the baby who wants to be held all the time, patience with your own body. Psalm 78 is an excellent perch as we look at the patience of God this week and draw encouragement from it. This psalm details how the people of Israel "forgot His works and His wonders that He had shown them (v. 11). The writer, Asaph, wrote that Israel tested, sinned, rebelled, demanded, spoke against, and forgot God (vv. 11–19). Yet God remained faithful to bring David to the throne (v. 70) and, through David, the line of the Savior that we know he represents.

Along the way, however, "Again and again they tempted God, and limited the Holy One of Israel" (78:41). And "yet he was merciful; he forgave their iniquities and did not destroy them. Time after time he restrained his anger and did not stir up his full wrath" (78:38 NIV). As mothers, we need to pay attention to this example of patience, which is quite often an act of great restraint, or self-control, in the face of just provocation. God's patience did not occur in a painless vacuum. Ours will not either. Patience with our babies is remembering that they are so very helpless. Patience with others is, in part, not stirring up more of the anger we may rightfully feel. We practice patient self-control, seeing how God is patient with us.

Patient for Repentance

The Lord is not slow in keeping his
promise, . . . Instead he is patient . . .
not wanting anyone to perish, but
everyone to come to repentance.

2 PETER 3:9 NIV

$\mathcal{T}$he apostles surely did not expect the second coming of God to be so long in coming. It's easy to imagine that Peter, James, John, and the others who heard Jesus say words like "A little while, and you will not see Me; and again a little while, and you will see Me" might have expected Christ's second coming to be like that "little while" they experienced in the three days between the cross and the empty tomb (John 16:16). They might have expected to see Jesus return to earth again in their lifetime. But as His return tarried, and still tarries today, how should we interpret His slowness?

If God is slow, it is not a slowness in keeping His promises. It is the slowness of patience and mercy. His coming will be an awesome and wonderful day. But it will also be an awful and terrible day for those who have not turned to Him in repentance and faith. So, every day that God tarries is one more day for a sinner to turn. It is one more chance for mercy. His slowness is a sign of His great love and His great longing—"not wanting anyone to perish, but everyone to come to repentance." Likewise, our aim in parenting must also be a great longing for our children's repentance, for their turning to Him. That may seem far away as you try to coax a burp out of your baby or perfect the art of putting Baby down without waking her. But it's never too early to understand that our role as mamas is to shepherd hearts in need of a Savior.

Active Patience

Rest in the LORD, and wait patiently
for Him; do not fret because of
him who prospers in his way.
PSALM 37:7

L ife with a two-month-old requires much patient waiting. We must wait for them to learn to sleep through the night, to feed, to work through crankiness or colic. Here in Psalm 37, we see an oft-repeated command: "wait patiently" for the Lord. In Hebrew, patient waiting is the active verb *chool*. The other fifty-nine times this verb is used in the Bible, it is translated with the words *whirl, twirl, dance,* or even *writhe.* This is an active waiting. There will be moments of pain and moments of pleasure within it, just like the ups and downs in expecting a baby during pregnancy.[1]

Notice David wrote this verse as a command. It was almost as if he was commanding himself to do the thing he needed to do: wait patiently for Him. In 1 Samuel 30:6, David "strengthened himself in the LORD." He was reminding himself of all the truths about God that he needed to hear to remain patient. Perhaps even writing and playing the psalms was his way of taking an active role waiting. Do you take an active role in encouraging yourself in the Lord? Perhaps we've mistaken patience as a passive trait for too long.

What have you had to wait for in your life? How has God shown you His mercy or purposes even in that waiting or because of that waiting?

What does your little one enjoy looking at these days? Does she have a special fascination for a mobile, enjoy looking at her own hands, or light up at your smile? What holds her gaze?

Monthly Memories
and Milestones

When did Baby smile for the first time? Who or what made your
little one smile?

How is Baby growing? Is Baby tall and lean or already getting
adorable rolls?

What special holidays have you celebrated since Baby's arrival? How did you celebrate? Did your little one wear a special outfit?

How is Baby sleeping these days? What helps your little one sleep?

Other moments or milestones from this month:

Your Three-Month-Old Developmental Guide

Congrats! Your baby has just completed the fourth trimester! Didn't know there was a fourth trimester? That's okay. It's a relatively new term, coined by Dr. Harvey Karp, to describe the first twelve weeks of life outside the womb. In these months, Baby is still doing so much developing, especially in terms of brain growth, that he says it is almost as if Baby needed another three months in utero. (I bet you're glad that God didn't share Dr. Karp's way of thinking!) The good news is that by three months lots of big changes have occurred for Baby, including big strides in brain development.

One of the biggest brain developments makes sleeping for longer stretches possible. As newborns, babies plunge directly into REM sleep, making them more likely to rouse and less likely to sleep for long stretches at a time. But by three to four months, baby sleep patterns are becoming more adult-like. Infants no longer fall right into REM after drifting off, and their sleep cycles begin to include longer stretches of slow-wave or "deep" sleep. This is good news for sleep-deprived mamas. However, when experts talk about Baby "sleeping through the night," they usually mean these longer stretches of five to six hours of sleep. This is not exactly what you may call sleeping through the night! Also, not all babies develop on the same timeline, and aside from being sleepy yourself, if your baby is not yet sleeping those longer stretches, they are in good company. By six months of age, 38 percent of babies still are not sleeping through the night.

There are more big changes to come in the months ahead. This month you can expect your baby to likely smile more and begin to have little "conversations" with you. By "conversation" I mean lots of back and forth smiling, coos, vocalizations, a few raspberries, and some hand gestures. These are great bonding moments!

You can also expect your baby to discover her hands this month. She may bring them up to her mouth and discover a thumb is perfect for sucking. She also may put her hands in front of her face and examine them with more fascination. Those hands will begin batting at things as her hand-eye coordination also grows. And she will open and shut fingers as she begins to learn how to grasp things.

Muscle control is also continuing to develop. By twelve weeks, most babies will hold their heads up at a 90-degree angle. And when supported under their arms, most will bear weight on their legs. These are two milestones your doctor may look for on this month's visit. Tummy time continues to be a crucial aid to your baby strengthening her core, which will be important over the months to come.

A God Who Is Everywhere

*Where can I go from your Spirit? Where
can I flee from your presence? If I go up
to the heavens, you are there; if I make
my bed in the depths, you are there.*
PSALM 139:7–8 NIV

$\mathcal{M}$ iddle-of-the-night feedings can be incredibly lonely. Amid exhaustion, you may feel frustrated with a baby who won't go back to sleep easily or who has reflux or wakes up too frequently. Your hard work may feel invisible; after all, no one else may be awake. While these feelings may come at night or during other times, remember that there is never a place or moment where God is not there with you. *If I get up in the night, You are there, God. If I make my bed in the nursery recliner, You are there. If I sit in the hallway to hear the church service because Baby is crying, You are there. If I stay home from the social event of the season because Baby isn't taking a bottle, even there Your hand will hold me.*

What a comfort to realize that God is present with us in every place and moment! What a comfort to know we are never truly alone! The God who is everywhere sees you. He feels compassion for you. And He wants to meet you in those lonely moments. He wants to comfort you there, fellowship with you there, and listen to your heart. What an invitation these lonely moments are to enjoy a deep intimacy with God! He sees you as no other, loves you as no other, shares in your triumphs and heartaches as no other. What a bond you can have when you realize He is there!

God with Us

*And the Word became flesh and dwelt
among us, and we beheld His glory,
the glory as of the only begotten of
the Father, full of grace and truth.*
JOHN 1:14

God is everywhere, but He is also right here with us. Throughout Scripture, we see this refrain of God being with His people. He led them by pillar of cloud by day and fire by night as they left Egypt (Exodus 13:21–22). He dwelt among them in the wilderness in a temporary tabernacle (Exodus 40:30). And not surprisingly, He revealed Himself as "God with us" in the person of Jesus Christ, our Immanuel, who "tabernacled" with us.

As moms in the postpartum phase, it's common to feel unlovely, lonely, or just lost in terms of our value, but our God wants us—He wants relationship with us. He wants to be with us. That thought alone should infuse us with value and worth. Jesus went to such incredible lengths to show us He is *with* us. Even though sin kept us apart from a holy God, He bore our sin so that God could be not only with us but also *for* us, as one who is on our side (Romans 8:31). These days as you hold your little one, let it remind you of how Jesus came as a baby to be our Immanuel. Through His nearness to us, we behold the glory of the Father. We behold a God who wants to draw near. As you hold your little one, let it lead you to behold the heart of the Father who wants to draw near to you.

At Hand and Far Off

"Am I a God near at hand," says the LORD,
*"And not a God afar off? Can anyone
hide himself in secret places, so I shall
not see him?" says the* LORD; *"Do I not
fill heaven and earth?" says the* LORD.
JEREMIAH 23:23–24

When I was first adjusting to life mothering more than one little person, I would often wish I were an octopus. I know that seems crazy. Bear with me. I'd think to myself, *If I had eight arms, I could comfort the crying baby and the toddler who just took a tumble. I could cook dinner and change the diaper.* You get the idea. If only I had a few more (super stretchy) arms, I could do it all. Well, in all seriousness, God never intended for me to be everywhere at once. He can do it; I can't.

So here's the thing about that. Motherhood often pushes us to feel our limitations. *I can't do this and this,* or *I can't be here and there.* Sometimes in our limitations, we let people down. That doesn't feel so great. Maybe it's an older sibling who is jealous because Mom's lap is occupied. Maybe it's a boss who's frustrated that you can't make it to the after-hours meet-and-greet. Or maybe it's a friend whose far-off wedding you can't attend because of Baby's needs. Eventually, we'll bump up against our limitations. We can either respond with a more desperate attempt to be everywhere and do everything better next time—leading to frustration—or we can embrace that God uses our limitations to teach others about His reach. He is everywhere and is even available to comfort the person whose needs I can't meet.

Your baby has reached the three-month mark! Are you doing anything fun to mark the months? Maybe a picture on a special blanket or chair? What special moments with Baby do you want to remember from recent weeks?

God is omnipresent, and you are not. How does this truth free you from worrying about your limitations as a mother?

El Shaddai

When Abram was ninety-nine years
old, the LORD appeared to Abram
and said to him, "I am Almighty God;
walk before Me and be blameless."
GENESIS 17:1

Have you ever sensed God preparing you for something? Perhaps God prepared you for meeting your spouse or becoming a mom by bringing just the right conversation, verse, or song to ready your heart for the new thing He wanted to do in your life. Well, when Abraham was nearly one hundred, God prepared him for the biggest news of his life by sharing one of His names for the very first time: El Shaddai, or Almighty God. This name signifies God's omnipotence—His all-powerful nature. And it was certainly no coincidence that God revealed Himself as the almighty God right before He told Abraham of His plan to give him and Sarah a baby.

Sarah and Abraham's first reaction to God's incredible plan? Laughter (Genesis 17:17; 18:12). Surely, there must be some mistake! But God had made no mistake. He'd prepared them for parenthood by sharing His name: the almighty God. And He reassured them with these words we love to quote: "Is anything too hard for the LORD?" (Genesis 18:14). That's a question we should let reverberate within our souls: there is nothing God cannot do. His power is not confined to the laws of physics or time. Nothing is too hard for God. What are you facing today with Baby that seems too hard? Is your milk supply low? Is Baby napping poorly? Are you finding it difficult to go back to work or stay home? Nothing is too hard for God. Bring your needs to Him with faith.

That Same Power

*. . . and his incomparably great power
for us who believe. That power is the
same as the mighty strength he exerted
when he raised Christ from the dead.*
EPHESIANS 1:19–20 NIV

This week we've been marveling at our all-powerful God, who is for us even in the midst of our needs as moms. Jesus showed that raw power. He banished demons, calmed storms, made lame men leap, and called the dead back to life. His earthly ministry demonstrated His power over the demonic realm, the natural elements, and physical ailments.

But the height of God's power on display was in the mighty work of raising Jesus from the dead. This man who had suffered a horrifically brutal torture and death, whose body lay lifeless for three days, whose tomb was sealed and guarded, came alive again—restored—not as a ghost but as a physical man. He ate and drank. He touched and embraced people. And He did this in a body that was not beaten and bruised, but fully renewed and transformed.

This alone is staggering to meditate on, but Paul told us in Ephesians that this same power that raised Jesus from the dead and seated Him in the heavenly realms is the power God has for us who believe. In Romans 8:11, Paul amplified this, writing that the same "Spirit of him who raised Jesus from the dead is living in you" (NIV). Isn't this a stunning thought? Where do you need to lay hold of that power today, Mama? Is the baby fussy at dinner time? Are you frustrated you can't get things done with Baby's needs? The power that raised Jesus from the dead is in you by the Spirit, infusing you with strength for this day. His power is alive in you!

Power in Weakness

But we have this treasure in jars of
clay to show that this all-surpassing
power is from God and not from us.
2 CORINTHIANS 4:7 NIV

This week, as we've considered God as the almighty One and as we've looked at what it means to have the same power that raised Jesus from the dead at work inside of us, you may be thinking that you are anything but powerful these days. As a sleep-deprived, energy-depleted mama of a tiny one, you acutely feel your weakness. You may also feel tied down physically, unable to serve in ways you were used to serving before.

And yet God delights in displaying His power in the things that seem weak and foolish. In the weakness of the cross, His power triumphed. In the frailty of fishermen, His gospel went forth. In beatings and hardships and persecutions, the church multiplied. What may look weak is often the most powerful thing of all.

So if you have a vague feeling that your current state of motherhood is neither productive nor powerful, look again with the eyes of faith. As you kneel down to change a soiled diaper, remember Jesus knelt down to wash the disciples' feet; as you gather your little one in your arms to feed him, remember that Jesus served by multiplying loaves and fish for the hungry crowds; and as you give your life for this little one day in and day out, remember Jesus' greatest display of power was in the so-called "weakness" of giving His life for His children.

Is anything too hard for the Lord? Remember a time in your life or in someone else's life when something seemed humanly too hard, but God still did it.

Dear little one, sometimes you make me laugh when you . . .

Gentle Shepherd

He will feed His flock like a shepherd;
He will gather the lambs with His arm,
and carry them in His bosom, and
gently lead those who are with young.
ISAIAH 40:11

This week we focus on the gentleness of God. As mothers of very young ones, this is a truth we so desperately need. Our God is gentle with us. He is not a harsh taskmaster. Like a kind and watchful shepherd, He tends His flock. He watches over them. He cares for them. The verb translated "to feed" denotes more than our word at present. It refers to all the care of a shepherd over his flock: tending, guarding, guiding, providing, and overseeing. This is our gentle God toward us.

This verse also highlights His special tenderness toward mothers with young. A shepherd knows that lambs are especially vulnerable to predators of all kinds. And a mother ewe needs extra gentle care as she moves along with the flock and tries to also nourish and protect her lamb. The shepherd is loving: He sees the weak lamb fall behind and naturally scoops it up in his arms. He holds it close to his heart. His loving care of the lamb is also proof of his love for the mother ewe. Oh mothers, can you hear in this verse God's great heart for you? He is not leading the mother lambs with a whip. He is the author of gentleness; trust that He will be gentle with you—likewise be gentle with yourself.

Hope in His Gentleness

*So the sisters sent word to Jesus,
"Lord, the one you love is sick."*
JOHN 11:3 NIV

What do you expect from God when you go to Him with your pain, your weariness, your need? During this time, when you can hardly keep your eyes open to pray or feel drained by the constant demands of caring for another or the strain of balancing work outside the home, do you expect Him to be angry with you for bothering Him with your needs? Do you expect Him to be annoyed at your pestering? Or do you expect kindness, gentleness, and grace? You may know the right answer, Mama, but how does your heart answer?

When Mary and Martha faced the deep heartache of their brother Lazarus's illness, they turned to Jesus. Sure, they had probably seen Him perform miracles before. But it was not His power they were counting on; it was His compassion. Martha would have remembered the gentle way He rebuked her when she had been too busy in the kitchen. They both would have remembered how gently He invited them to learn. So they sent word to Jesus that "the one you love is sick." Note well: it's not "the one who loves you" but rather "the one you love." This reminds us that it is His faithful love that matters, not our faltering love. Jesus was gentle with the too-busy, gentle in His invitation to fellowship, gentle when accused of arriving too late. Martha and Mary banked on Jesus' gentleness: we can too.

Fight for Gentleness

But you, O man of God, flee these things
and pursue righteousness, godliness,
faith, love, patience, gentleness.
Fight the good fight of faith.
1 TIMOTHY 6:11–12

I love the juxtaposition in today's verse of gentleness and fight. The two words could not be more opposite. And yet right at the center of this charge from Paul to Timothy is the injunction to pursue gentleness to fight the good fight of faith. Gentleness is often dismissed by the world as weakness. "Don't be a doormat!" the world says; true strength is speaking up for your rights, asserting your needs, and taking matters into your own hands. For Paul, however, the virtues in this verse were far from weakness. These were signs of power—power bent in the form of submission to the King. They were virtues worth fighting for.

For most moms, gentleness comes easily with Baby. But what can the gentle care that comes easily with this tiny one teach us about how to fight for gentleness with people who are not so easy to love? With the mother-in-law who hurts your feelings, the boss who doesn't appreciate your effort, the friend who betrays your trust? With our babies, we are quick to recognize their weakness, but with others we expect perfection. With those who are harder to love, we have to fight to recognize that like us, they are weak. We have to struggle to remember our identity is in Christ, not in their opinion of us. We have to strive to lay down our rights for the sake of loving them more than ourselves.

What does it mean to you to be reminded that God carries the lambs next to His heart? What comfort does this give you as you think about your baby?

Dear Baby, I hope you never forget . . .

Unfathomable Wisdom

*Oh, the depth of the riches both of
the wisdom and knowledge of God!
How unsearchable are His judgments
and His ways past finding out!*
ROMANS 11:33

Have you stopped to consider the marvels of God's wisdom in your baby? Even moments after birth, you may have noticed a reflex called rooting. If you stroked Baby's cheek, he would turn toward you with a sucking motion. He responds to embrace with his heart rate and breathing slowing down. His marvelous brain is born with hundreds of billions of brain cells, and the cortex's smooth surface will crinkle to keep pace with the astonishing growth of the first three years. If there is so much wisdom in the creature, how much more astonishing is the unfathomable mind of the Creator!

So what is the wisdom of God? Wisdom has an element of both knowledge and moral understanding. There is no lack in God's wisdom. As the psalmist declared, "His understanding is infinite" (Psalm 147:5). He knows everything: men's thoughts (Ezekiel 11:5; Luke 5:21–22), the future, and every eventuality under any set of circumstances (1 Samuel 23:10–12; 2 Kings 8:10). It is not possible for God to fail to bring His purposes to their proper end. His wisdom is fully supported by His omniscience.

But His wisdom is also fully good. It is a righteous wisdom. As James wrote, this wisdom is "first pure, then peaceable, gentle, willing to yield, full of mercy and good fruits, without partiality and without hypocrisy" (James 3:17). We can fully trust this wisdom because it is perfect in knowledge and righteousness, infinite and freely given!

Higher Ways

*"For My thoughts are not your
thoughts, nor are your ways My ways,"
says the LORD. "For as the heavens
are higher than the earth, so are My
ways higher than your ways, and My
thoughts than your thoughts."*

ISAIAH 55:8–9

$\mathcal{D}$id you know that babies are not born with the ability to see depth? It is not until around five months that they begin to form a three-dimensional picture of the world.[1] It's hard to imagine what the world would look like without depth; we are so accustomed to seeing with it. But in a real sense, we are seeing the world around us with more comprehension, not only visually but on the cognitive level as well. Just as there is a huge gap between a baby's understanding of the world and our own, how much greater is the gap between our "vision" and God's?

No wonder, as God explained to the prophet Isaiah, "My thoughts are not your thoughts, nor are your ways My ways" (Isaiah 55:8). Aren't we glad that God's thoughts are not ours? If God thought like we do, His ways would be subject to sin and selfishness; they would be confined by limited knowledge. Would I really want a God like that?

God's thoughts are higher (Isaiah 55:9). He sees the entire story and knows how it all began and how it all will end. He knows how He will work every evil act committed in the world together for good. He knows how to use every iota of human history to bring about His glory. Don't we want to trust that kind of omniscient and holy God to answer our prayers?

Walking in Wisdom

Trust in the LORD with all your heart, and
lean not on your own understanding.
PROVERBS 3:5

*B*elieve it or not, although walking is a good nine months to a year away for your infant, she is now laying the foundation for that skill: raising her head off the ground, developing core body strength, and growing in coordination. Before we walk in wisdom, we need to have a foundation in place. "The fear of the LORD is the beginning of knowledge" (Proverbs 1:7). Wisdom cannot begin anywhere except in reverence and awe for God, in submission to His will. We gain wisdom through obedience. As we submit ourselves to His Word, He enables us to learn the ways of wisdom.

When your little one begins to walk, she will start by first cruising—holding on to anything nearby to steady herself as she gains mastery. Likewise for us, wisdom also takes its first steps holding on. "Trust in the LORD with all your heart, and lean not on your own understanding" (Proverbs 3:5). We hold to the Word, like that little one will hold on to furniture, a hand, or anything else for dear life. But while your baby will eventually let go, we do not. Wisdom walks with a lifelong lean—leaning on God's understanding.

Did you know that when infants are learning to walk, they average about seventeen falls per hour? You will make mistakes, too, as you grow in wisdom. But by grace, you will fall into the Father's loving arms and get back up because He cheers you on.

Who in your life embodies many of the qualities of wisdom?
What aspects of this person are worthy of imitation?

Write a prayer for your baby to one day walk in the ways of
wisdom.

Monthly Memories and Milestones

Who does Baby get most excited to see?

_____

_____

_____

_____

What other special people are in Baby's life right now?

_____

_____

_____

_____

_____

What special seasonal activities has Baby enjoyed?

_____

_____

_____

_____

_____

What were the circumstances surrounding Baby's first laugh?

What other special moments do you want to remember from this month that has passed?

Your Four-Month-Old Developmental Guide

Good news! This month, life may begin to feel more settled for you and your infant. By four months your baby's eating and sleeping habits will tend to become more predictable. This will help you feel more balanced and rested.

This month may also be a time when developmental milestones become more pronounced. Most four-month-olds will be able to

- Coordinate movement from hands to mouth
- Roll from front to back
- Follow objects with eyes from side to side
- See something they want and grasp for it
- Sit with support
- Reach for objects with one hand
- Bear weight when supported and standing on a hard surface
- Hold up head and chest
- Hold a rattle or other baby toys
- Push up to elbows when lying on stomach
- Cry in various ways to communicate needs
- Recognize people from a distance
- Babble and try to mimic language, like cooing
- Mimic expressions like frowning or smiling

Remember that all babies reach milestones at different rates. Talk to your pediatrician about any concerns you might have. But if there are reasons for concern, finding an online or in-person support group can help you feel less alone and provide resources. Whatever your baby's developmental curve, celebrate him, remembering every child is precious and made in the image of God.

As babies develop the ability to roll over, grasp objects, and instinctively put items in their mouths, parents need to be more proactive in removing dangerous or tiny objects from within reach. Choking is the leading cause of death among children under four years of age. Here is a handy test anyone can do: if the object can fit through a toilet paper roll, it's something that could be a choking hazard for your baby and is best removed from reach.

Agape Love

Beloved, let us love one another, for love is of God; and everyone who loves is born of God and knows God. He who does not love does not know God, for God is love.

1 JOHN 4:7–8

$\mathcal{M}$ ost attributes of God are adjectives. But there are a few nouns used to describe God (light, life, and truth, for example). Of course, God is loving. But Scripture takes it one step further. It says that God is love itself. He is agape, all-giving love. This is His nature, and this is the first cause for our imitative loves. As mothers, we reflect Him in His agape love when we love our babies selflessly, expecting nothing in return. We reflect Him when we love sacrificially. And we reflect Him when we love lavishly, generously pouring out time, attention, and resources for Baby, a spouse, and others.

Instinctively, we know that love changes things. But we may not realize how deeply it affects our children. A recent study measured a child's brain growth in conjunction with the nurturing support given by the mother or caregiver. The study found that children with supportive, nurturing mothers in the preschool years had a hippocampus significantly greater in volume when measured again at ages six to thirteen.[1] Another study of premature infants found that those who were exposed to their mothers' voices and heartbeat sounds in the incubator had stronger patterns of brain growth.[2] Our love, our support, our voice—all matter to our children. We have an opportunity to reflect the God of love to our children, and that love changes them, not only in terms of their brains but forever. God gifts us love so that we may gift love to others.

A Sacrificial Love

In this the love of God was manifested
toward us, that God has sent His
only begotten Son into the world,
that we might live through Him.

1 JOHN 4:9

As we continue to look at God as love this week, we wade further into 1 John 4. What does agape love look like? God answers here with the frame around the ultimate act of self-sacrifice: Jesus giving His own life. Jesus drank to the dregs the full cup of God's wrath so that we do not have to touch it. He bore the full weight of sin's condemnation and the ultimate abandonment of God. And He did this not because of any need on His part, not for self-fulfillment or as a fleeting act of emotion. It was a choice of selfless love. It stands as the ultimate picture of agape love. And this, John said, is how *we* ought to love *one another* (4:11).

As mothers we have many important lessons to learn here: we are to love without desiring to manipulate gain. Our children are not our trophies or our levers to fulfill *our* dreams. *We* are to love on purpose, not on whim. There will be times when love will not come naturally to us—when baby wakes prematurely from a nap when we were about to have a moment to ourselves, when a defiant two-year-old yells "no," or when a preschooler is still wetting the bed at night. Agape love changes us. It transforms us into a people willing to love even if it means we must suffer for the other. This ultimate act of God's love for us becomes the wellspring of the gift-love He wants to see flow from us in surrendered worship.

Perfected Love

No one has seen God at any time. If we love one another, God abides in us, and His love has been perfected in us.
1 JOHN 4:12

*G*od, who needed nothing, created out of the joy of His being. His perfect Trinitarian love overflowed in the days of creation and, at its apex, in the creation of man and woman. But the Bible doesn't say this creative act was the perfection or completion of God's love. Instead, God's love is perfected in us as we love one another. Today, you have a chance for the fullness of God's love to be made complete as it inspires you to give without expecting anything in return. The perfected love in us gives us boldness on the Day of Judgment because we know that such love is not human, but divine. In other words, it is not of us. Such love comes only in abiding in God and having His Spirit create this fruit.

What does it mean to abide in God and for Him to abide in us? This is a deliberate act of keeping our thoughts fixed on Jesus, of staying relationally close to God through an open and ongoing prayer life, through a lifestyle of repentance and faith. In the minutiae of life, as you dress baby, thanking God for this gift of wonder; as you change a diaper, thanking God for an opportunity to serve; as you rock that tiny one, talking to God about your day. And here's the beautiful thing, though "no one has seen God at any time," as verse 12 reminds us, the beauty of the invisible God becomes visible in this world through acts of love. We have a chance to make invisible realities visible in our homes today.

Write a prayer for you and your little one to grow in love for God and others.

About a year ago, you discovered you were pregnant. What was that like? How did you share the news with those dearest to you?

Life

For as the Father has life in himself, so he has granted the Son also to have life in himself.
JOHN 5:26 NIV

Four months ago, God brought a miracle into your arms that has something specific to teach you about who He is. That miracle? Life. While life is a fundamental aspect of the nature of God, it is also one we barely talk about. God "the Father has life in himself" (John 5:26). What are the implications of this? If we were to go on a quest for the source of life, it would lead directly to God. He is the fountainhead, the wellspring. No other creature can be said to have life in this way. But God has granted His Son to have life and to *give* life. That is why Jesus calls Himself the Bread of Life (John 6:35); the living water (John 7:38); the way, the truth, and the life (John 14:6); and "the author of life" (Acts 3:15 NIV). It is life that is really central here. Jesus, like God the Father, is life in Himself, and He gives life.

When you look at the living, breathing, moving, willful miracle of life before you, what does God want to teach you about Himself? Perhaps that He is the power that animates every living thing. He is breath, will, intention, word, growth, and creativity. He is the antithesis of death because death is the absence of love, compassion, mercy, goodness, justice, gentleness, and gratitude. He sent Jesus into the world, in part, to destroy death for this reason and to offer us that quality that is Himself: life everlasting, life abundant, life overflowing.

Everlasting Life

*And this is eternal life, that they
know you, the only true God, and
Jesus Christ whom you have sent.*

JOHN 17:3 ESV

Not so long ago that little one was brand new to you. Now you know each other intimately; you know her cries, her expressions, her favorite way to sleep, and what makes her smile. In a blink, she has changed. Blink again, and she will be a curious preschooler asking, "Why is this?" and "How is that?" Blink again, and she will be a teenager asking you tough questions. Questions like "What is the meaning of life?" Will you know how to respond?

Jesus says that life is more than just food and clothing (Luke 12:22). It's more than our calling, more than our relationships, more than mere happiness. He says that eternal life is to know "the only true God, and Jesus Christ whom [God has] sent" (John 17:3). Abundant life, everlasting life can begin now, on this side of physical death, because eternal life is *knowing God*. As you teach your little one to know and love God, you are investing in them for all eternity. A soul is a weighty thing, and God has given you such a high and holy calling as a mother. While only the Spirit draws a person to salvation, you can till the spiritual soil, plant seeds, water, and weed. To know God—this is eternal life. What a holy vocation we mothers have! Let us never disparage the day of small things!

Overflowing Life

Everyone who drinks of this water will
be thirsty again, but whoever drinks of
the water that I will give him will never
be thirsty again. The water that I will
give him will become in him a spring
of water welling up to eternal life.
JOHN 4:13–14 ESV

Oh, sweet mama friend, I know deeply that this life of mothering is an exhausting one. Some days I feel like I do nothing but give, from Baby's first morning cry until the moment I flop down in bed at night. While I love the life I live, it is a life of continual service and sacrifice. Where can we draw the strength to keep on giving with joy? You will run dry—burn out—if you don't draw from a well deeper than yourself.

Jesus promised us that as we drink from Him, we will not grow thirsty again. Instead, we will overflow. He promised, "The water that I will give him will become in him a spring of water welling up to eternal life" (John 4:14 ESV). He also said, "Whoever believes in me, as the Scripture has said, 'Out of his heart will flow rivers of living water'" (7:38 ESV). As we are connected to Jesus, we are satiated. He fills us to overflowing that we may overflow. We can give and keep on giving because He satisfies us. Overflowing life is one of the secrets of mothering well. Jesus is the key. He gives us joy in pouring ourselves out, such that it doesn't feel like a sacrifice but a privilege.

Who shows special affection for your baby? Is there a relative, sibling, or friend from church who is always especially glad to see your infant?

Abundant life—how do you think the world defines this? What is God's view of abundant life?

The Independence of God

*The God who made the world and
everything in it, being Lord of heaven
and earth, does not live in temples made
by man, nor is he served by human
hands, as though he needed anything,
since he himself gives to all mankind
life and breath and everything.*

ACTS 17:24–25 ESV

*D*o you feel like you can't complete a task without an interruption—a diaper blowout, an older child melting down, or someone already hungry for the next meal? Here's a freeing thought amid your state of overwhelm: God doesn't need you. Yes, He has chosen to use you. He has made you with a purpose, but if you cannot even get out of bed today or find all you "accomplish" is a load of laundry, He will still make the sun rise and set, and He will accomplish all His holy will.

God's independence or self-sufficiency points to the fact that God is completely sufficient in and of Himself. He does not need us. He does not need creation. Yet He made us and all created things, and we can bring Him joy and glory. It points us back to the joy and perfect harmony of the Trinity that existed before time. God's self-sufficiency may seem like a strange truth to focus on devotionally. But it is really freeing. God created not out of loneliness or need but out of love and joy. He calls us to join into His work, not because He is incapable of doing it Himself but because He wants to share the joy with us.

God's Independence and Our Dependence

I am the vine; you are the branches.
If you remain in me and I in you,
you will bear much fruit; apart
from me you can do nothing.
JOHN 15:5 NIV

In most of God's attributes, we seek to be like Him, right? But as we learned in yesterday's devotion, God is completely independent or self-sufficient. He does not need anything from man or creation, but creates and calls us for His joy and glory. Are we supposed to imitate Him in this self-sufficiency? No. Jesus stated clearly that we are completely and utterly dependent.

Here are a few ways we need God. We need His Spirit to give us understanding (1 Corinthians 2:12). We need His power to do His will (1 Corinthians 2:1–5). We need strength to endure in everything He calls us to do (2 Thessalonians 1:11). We need His strength to speak and serve (1 Peter 4:11). We need Him for breath, being, and movement (Acts 17:28). In short, we need Him for everything.

Too often we turn to God when we've tried in our own strength and come up short. Instead, God wants us to embrace our dependence, to come to Him from the beginning, not when we are at our end. David gave us a good example of this: "Be my strong refuge, to which I may resort continually" (Psalm 71:3). He rightly saw an ongoing need for God. As that little baby in your arms looks to you for every comfort and protection, so should you look to God for every need.

God's Independence and Our Meaning

In Him also we have obtained an inheritance, . . . that we who first trusted in Christ should be to the praise of His glory.
EPHESIANS 1:11–12

*W*hen we talk about God's independence or self-sufficiency, it is easy to assume that since God does not need us, our existence is meaningless. But nothing could be further from the truth. Scripture plainly teaches that although God needs nothing, He chose to create us for His glory and enjoyment, so that we could glorify Him and experience the deep joy of closeness with Him for eternity. He chose to infuse our lives with meaning, bringing both glory and joy to Him. And one of the purposes He has set for you is to mother your little one.

In Ephesians, Paul told us we were predestined for a purpose: for "the praise of His glory." One of the beautiful purposes for which you were created is to nurture and love the child before you—as you do you bring Him glory. Through the prophet Isaiah, God gave us a vivid word picture of this concept. God said, "You shall be a crown of glory in the hand of the LORD, and a royal diadem in the hand of your God" (Isaiah 62:3). Our redeemed lives crown the Creator with splendor. He continued, "My Delight Is in Her" (Isaiah 62:4–5 ESV). Doesn't it take your breath away? Let us hold fast to this soul-satisfying truth. Your calling as a mother, and the other roles to which He has called you, matter deeply to God. Because we are significant to Him, our lives are full of meaning, value, and worth.

What comfort is there for us in God's self-sufficiency?

_____

_____

_____

_____

_____

_____

By taking care of your baby's daily needs, you model God's total care for us. While your little one will not remember this time, he is learning to feel safe in that total care. Write to your baby about how you care for him now and the joy you take in that care.

_____

_____

_____

_____

_____

_____

_____

God's Unchanging Nature

Of old You laid the foundation of the earth, and the heavens are the work of Your hands. They will perish, but You will endure; yes, they will all grow old like a garment; like a cloak You will change them, and they will be changed. But You are the same, and Your years will have no end.

PSALM 102:25–27

In our lives, change is a constant. Our little ones are changing daily: pushing themselves up, rolling, smiling, cooing, and laughing. Soon they will be sitting up and starting on solids. Like a gently flowing stream, the motion is continuous, mesmerizing.

Imagine standing and looking at a mountain. Your job is to stand and watch for change—not change to the trees and their leaves, but change to the mountain itself. You'd be there a while, right? The psalmist in today's verses contrasted God's unchanging nature with things in his environment that seemed permanent. The earth and the sky certainly seem permanent. Yet, compared to God, they are like a piece of clothing, one day new but soon spoiled with spit-up, fit for the laundry heap. In comparison with God, even our most timeless creations—mountains, skies, seas—are a stream of constant motion. One day He will change them out, but God is eternal, everlasting, and unchanging.

Before the foundations of the earth, He was. And long after the heavens and earth perish, God will be. Because of this, we can be confident that His plans, His purposes, and His promises will not change for us. We can trust the One who is unchanging.

God's Unchanging Promises

*"Remember the former things of old,
for I am God, and there is no other;
I am God, and there is none like Me,
declaring the end from the beginning,
and from ancient times things that are
not yet done, saying, 'My counsel shall
stand, and I will do all My pleasure.'"*

ISAIAH 46:9–10

$\mathcal{A}$s mamas of infants, we are familiar with plans falling through. You plan to meet another mom for coffee at 10:00 a.m., only to have a diaper blowout on the way out the door. You plan to get up early to go for a jog, but Baby has kept you up all night, and instead, you hit snooze.

Unlike us, God's plans and promises cannot be thwarted. He is eternal; He exists outside of time and so can declare "the end from the beginning." Because He is God, "and there is no other," He is able from "ancient times" to have His plans and counsels stand. He is able and "will do all [His] pleasure."

What confidence does this give us? We can trust that "he who began a good work in you will carry it on to completion" (Philippians 1:6 NIV). We can trust that the Lord will come again just as He promised (1 Thessalonians 4:16–17). We can trust that He will never leave us nor forsake us (Deuteronomy 31:6). We can trust that He is working all things together for good for His children (Romans 8:28). These promises are firm, sure, and unchanging because God is firm, sure, and unchanging. What hope this gives us!

God Is Unchanging;
We Are Becoming

Do not conform to the pattern of
this world, but be transformed by
the renewing of your mind.
ROMANS 12:2 NIV

One of the joys of these early days of life with your little one is seeing his personality emerge. I'm sure you are already seeing little signs of your baby's personality: whether he likes being held or prefers blanket-time independence, whether he loves to babble or quietly observe, whether he loves noise and people or prefers quiet and calm. For the better part of the next two decades, you will have a front-row seat to the wonder of your little one becoming—your little one in process.

Likewise, while God's perfections and nature are complete and unchanging, you and I are everyday in the process of becoming. We are not yet what we will be. First John 3:2 says, "It has not yet been revealed what we shall be." John hinted that our transformation in Christ will be so breathtaking that we can't even fully imagine it yet. Just as you can hardly imagine the wonders of this baby in your arms as a grown man or woman, to an even greater degree the wonders of who we will become are veiled to us. But one day, "we shall be like Him, for we shall see Him as He is" (1 John 3:2). You are already cooperating with God in this metamorphosis by taking time in this book and in His Word to renew your minds (Romans 12:2), by contemplating His attributes, and by offering yourself as a "living sacrifice" (Romans 12:1). As we behold His wonder, we are becoming like Him.

What assurance is there for you as your remember that God is unchanging? How does this attribute give you confidence and peace?

What little glimpses of your baby's personality are you already observing?

Monthly Memories and Milestones

What are some of Baby's favorite toys right now?

_____

_____

_____

_____

_____

_____

_____

What are some special places you have visited with Baby?

_____

_____

_____

_____

_____

_____

_____

What is Baby's favorite way to get around these days? Car seat, baby carrier, stroller . . . ?

What is Baby's happiest time of day?

Other moments or milestones from this month:

Your Five-Month-Old Developmental Guide

$\mathcal{D}$ ouble the size, double the fun: your little wonder either has or soon will reach that big milestone of doubling his birth weight. While things slow down a little in terms of growth at this point (it will take him six more months to triple his birth weight), there are still plenty of fun milestones right around the corner.

Peekaboo anyone? Between four and seven months, your baby is likely still mastering what developmental experts call "object permanence." Object permanence is the understanding that something is still there when hidden or obscured. This is why peekaboo is such a thrill for infants of this age. They are genuinely surprised when you suddenly appear from behind your hands or from behind a blanket. It's also why hide-and-seek games are such a great brain-building activity for your little.

Babies may also begin to exhibit separation anxiety at this time. As they develop the realization that objects and people exist even when we can't see them, they begin to think that when they can't see Mom or Dad, they've gone away. Since their concept of time is still forming, they may become upset by their absence. At this age, whether Mom is in the kitchen, the bedroom, or away at the grocery store or work, it is all the same. To combat separation anxiety, it's best to have a consistent routine when leaving and to remain calm and upbeat. It also helps to leave when your baby is settled and fed rather than irritable, tired, or hungry.

Speaking of hungry, your little one may be getting near another milestone: beginning to experiment with solid foods. *Experiment* really is a good word for it at this point because early forays into eating solids are more about gaining experience with different textures and tastes than they are about acquiring nutrients. The bulk of your baby's nutritional needs will continue to be met by a steady diet of breastmilk or formula. But get the camera ready, and expect the unexpected when it is time to give baby a go at solids. She may love it or hate it. And whatever her reaction, remember that learning to eat solids is a process that takes time.

Time and experience are also what your infant needs these days as she masters the art of sitting upright and begins the wiggles and stretches that will ultimately lead to rolling, scooting, and crawling. Babies develop these skills according to their own developmental timelines, so don't worry if your baby is slow on the get-go. Enjoy the fact that your baby is stationary for a little while longer. After all, once baby gets going, there is no telling what he will get into!

Our Zealous God

Thus says the LORD of hosts: "I am zealous for Zion with great zeal; with great fervor I am zealous for her."
ZECHARIAH 8:2

As moms, we are passionate about our babies. There is nothing we won't do for them. If we hear that classical music makes them smarter, we crank up the "Baby Mozart." If experts say tummy time makes them stronger, we lie on the floor with them, giving them personal-trainer, tummy-time pep talks. We are zealous for our children; we have a focused desire for their welfare characterized by passion and commitment. We may not use the word *zeal* today, but as moms we instinctively understand it. Mama bears will do anything for their cubs.

Repeatedly, the Bible describes God as zealous for His people. His zeal is His passionate commitment to us. When it comes to us, no mountain is too high to scale, no obstacle too big to be torn down, no cost too great to suffer. Zechariah explained God's great fervor for us. He longs to dwell with us. Wonder of wonders, He wants to be with us. Often His zeal is attached to bringing back a remnant of His people (2 Kings 19:31; Isaiah 37:32). And here in Zechariah, we see that theme repeated: "Behold, I will save My people from the land of the east and from the land of the west; I will bring them back" (8:7–8). Why is God zealous for His people? He longs to be with them—to dwell in their midst. And He longs to see them flourish: "I am determined to do good to Jerusalem and to the house of Judah. Do not fear" (Zechariah 8:15). God is zealous for you.

Christ's Consuming Zeal

*And He said to those who sold doves,
"Take these things away! Do not
make My Father's house a house of
merchandise!" Then His disciples
remembered that it was written, "Zeal
for Your house has eaten Me up."*

JOHN 2:16–17

Maybe you have a T-shirt with the words "Mama Bear" on the front. It's a common epithet for moms and hints at how we mothers will do most anything to protect our "cubs." It is said that the most dangerous place a human can be in the wild is between a mama bear and her cubs. That mother bear is zealous for her offspring.

Some people are uncomfortable with the picture we have here of Jesus overturning tables to drive money changers from the temple. It is quite a different picture we see of Jesus from the gentle healer and thoughtful teacher. Who is this man brandishing a braided whip? Perhaps if you had only seen the soft side of a mother bear, you might also be surprised at her ability to be suddenly aggressive when danger confronts her brood.

Likewise, Jesus is zealous for the purity of His Father's house. It's not just that it is a holy place, though it is. It is the purpose for which it was made. It was made to be the place where God dwells with man. It was made to be "a house of prayer," not a "den of thieves" (Matthew 21:13). No wonder Jesus was angry. Someone had come between His people meeting with His Father. Jesus is zealous for His people to be able to draw near to the Father.

From Lukewarm to Zealous

*As many as I love, I rebuke and chasten.
Therefore be zealous and repent.*
REVELATION 3:19

In life with Baby, sometimes lukewarm is the goal. How many times have I sat beside the tub waiting for the water to reach that perfect temperature? How often have I labored over soup with my older kids, waiting for that perfect Goldilocks point: not too hot and not too cold—just right.

But when it comes to our faith, our God finds lukewarm revolting. In the letter to the church of Laodicea, Jesus rebuked the church for being neither hot nor cold (Revelation 3:15). He wished that they were at least one or the other. And He painted a rather graphic picture for us of just how revolting their lukewarm faith was: it made Him want to spew them out of His mouth (v. 16). This is a picture of a church that is trying hard to be middle-of-the-road, not too crazy about Jesus, but not ready to totally dump Him either: wanting His benefits without any of the pains or persecutions. It is a comfortable Christianity. And Jesus says He has no use for such revolting fare.

Zeal is the opposite. Zeal is a focused desire characterized by passionate commitment. Someone who is zealous for Christ will be hard to miss. We call these people "on fire for God" for good reason. It is a passionate, consuming, burning love of God that drives them. God wants zeal: holy passion for Him. And if we don't have it, the only zealous response is repentance (v. 19).

God is passionately committed to you. He longs to be with you. His heart is to see you flourish. Write a prayer of thanksgiving to God for His zealous heart for you.

Does your baby like bath time? What are Baby's favorite and not so favorite parts?

The Posture of Humility

*Have this mind among yourselves, which
is yours in Christ Jesus, who, though he
was in the form of God, did not count
equality with God a thing to be grasped,
but emptied himself, by taking the form of a
servant, being born in the likeness of men.*
PHILIPPIANS 2:5–7 ESV

When you said "yes" to motherhood, that meant sometimes saying "no" or at least "not right now" to parts of yourself. A lot of people have no idea about the things you've turned down: the promotion; the spotlight; the time, energy, and availability for that quiet dream of yours. Sometimes saying "yes" to motherhood has meant saying "no" or "later" to so much. I want you to know there is One who knows and who values the service in obscurity.

Christ is our example of the "no" of love. Though equality with God belonged to Him, though angels' praise was the glory He deserved, He willingly left it. He laid it aside—not forever, but for a season. And He emptied Himself. He took the form of a servant, and by so doing He set for us the ultimate example of love and greatness.

That doesn't mean that as mothers we have to give up our dreams. It means that as we dream our dreams, they are going to take on a God-shaped bent. They will be dreams shaped in the form of exalting Christ. Those dreams are ones that often have us stooping low in service because God's kingdom is an upside-down kingdom. We stoop to rise. We serve to lead. We die to live.

The Confidence of Humility

*Jesus, knowing that the Father had
given all things into His hands, and
that He had come from God and was
going to God, rose from supper . . . and
began to wash the disciples' feet.*

JOHN 13:3–5 ESV

Where do you find your identity? It's not an easy question. If this is your first baby, you may be discovering that some of the things that defined you in the past no longer exist. If you are staying at home with your little one, you may wonder who you truly are apart from work and social connections. If you are balancing work and baby, your identity may be in flux in a new way as you learn to wear both hats.

While God has given us roles and gifts, He wants our identity to be in something deeper. He wants our identity to be in *whose* we are. And if we belong to Christ, our identity is in Him. In this passage Jesus knew that He had been given everything. This gave Him confidence to give. He also knew that His destiny was not one of perpetual humiliation but ultimately of exaltation.

Jesus modeled for us how the security of our identity can fuel our service. Everything comes of God; therefore, we can be generous. We also know that we belong to God and that one day we will return to Him. We know that He sees and rewards our acts done in quiet service to Him. Humility flourishes when we are secure in Him.

A Coming Exaltation

Whoever exalts himself will be humbled, and he who humbles himself will be exalted.

MATTHEW 23:12

The kingdom of God is not like the kingdom of man. The way up is down. We lead by serving. We must decrease to increase. The least is the greatest. The inside and not the outside matters. It should not surprise us then that God's path to exaltation is not the path of the world. The world says that to be known you have to exalt yourself. The Bible says, "Humble yourselves in the sight of the Lord, and He will lift you up" (James 4:10).

This is good news for the quiet, often unglamorous service of motherhood. But what reward awaits the meek and humble? A sure and definite exaltation is waiting. Not only do we have the promise of Jesus in Matthew 23:12, but Peter said very similar words: "Humble yourselves, therefore, under the mighty hand of God so that at the proper time he may exalt you" (1 Peter 5:6 ESV). In the Sermon on the Mount, Jesus said that the meek will inherit the earth. So when we imitate Jesus and take on the form of a servant (whether in our mothering or unassuming service to the community or body of Christ), when we humble ourselves, when we give it all away, we do not do this because we are masochists. There is a reward coming. A day is coming when hidden service will be revealed. Paul told us that our works will be revealed by fire, and if it survives, that builder will receive a reward (1 Corinthians 3:13–14). That reward will be a lot more satisfying than a Mother's Day card and a bouquet of flowers. We work with an eye toward a future kingdom where our quiet acts of service do not go unnoticed by our Servant King.

Humility and service go hand in hand. Yet sometimes we serve for the praise of men. The Bible says that when we do this we already have received our reward (Matthew 6:2). Sometimes we serve because we are trying to earn favor with God. (Hint: we can't earn God's favor. That's why we need Jesus.) Write a prayer asking God to give you the right motivation to serve.

Write a prayer for your baby to grow to possess a servant's heart and true humility.

A Healing Light

This is the message we have heard from him and proclaim to you, that God is light, and in him is no darkness at all.

1 JOHN 1:5 ESV

When I was feeling sick as a teenager, I'd often stretch out in the sun on the patio and close my eyes. There was something soothing in the sun's rays. I didn't know then that T-lymphocytes are boosted by UVA light and that these direct our body's immune response to infectious micro-organisms. As little as five to ten minutes of sun exposure boosts the immune system.

In the Bible, one of the metaphors for God is that He is light. Many aspects of light remind us of God. Perhaps the most obvious, though, is that light is goodness. There is no darkness, or sin, at all in light. To be in this light is to experience the ultimate healing touch, to feel the warmth of God's goodness surround us. To walk in the light does not mean to walk in perfection. It means to walk in repentance and faith. As mothers, this is freeing. We are going to sin and mess up, especially in this difficult journey of child-rearing. But knowing that we don't have to try to hide our sin from God, but can run to Him and confess, is deep relief. As we openly bring the light to our sin and even confess our faults before our children, we model for them how God wants to bring light to our darkness. We model for them a love of the light because light brings the healing we need.

Light on the Offense

*The light shines in the darkness, and
the darkness has not overcome it.*

JOHN 1:5 ESV

$\mathcal{M}$ amas, I know some days you feel discouraged. You may feel like our culture is moving further from Jesus. Like me, you may worry what kind of world our children will have to live in. On these days we must try to lift our eyes and put our experience into perspective. And today's verse is a good place to start.

Jesus came into the world during an extremely dark time in history. So dark that it had been four hundred years since a prophetic word had come from God. Israel was under the oppressive rule of Rome. And the Roman-appointed King Herod was so wicked that he ordered all male babies age two and under to be killed, just to keep his political position.

But Christ came into this dark world to bring light. And here is the part that gives me so much hope: that light is advancing. In the early days of Christianity, when Peter and John were arrested and angels freed them from prison, one of the Jewish leaders, Gamaliel, gave this stunning advice: "If this plan or this work is of men, it will come to nothing; but if it is of God, you cannot overthrow it—lest you even be found to fight against God" (Acts 5:38–39). In the two thousand years since then, the light of Christ has been advancing. Though they persecuted the apostles, that light went forth. Though the early martyrs faced lions and were burned at the stake, the light advanced. Despite plagues, dark ages, inquisitions, and heretics, the light advanced. This movement is of God, and nothing can overthrow it. The light is on the offense, and it will prevail.

Passing the Torch

You are the light of the world. A city
that is set on a hill cannot be hidden.
MATTHEW 5:14

Sometimes I wonder if the early days of motherhood are filled with exhaustion for a purpose. We are continually reminded we are not enough; we *can't* do it all on our own. Jesus knew we weren't ready for the enormous responsibility of being the light of the world, even the light of our homes. To be radiant we need help. We need the Holy Spirit. And that is indeed what He left the disciples. And just in case we needed a visible sign of Him passing the torch, when the Holy Spirit came upon the disciples, it looked like tongues of fire (Acts 2:3). Jesus sent us light so that we could be the light, so that His light would radiate from within us.

Now we have this privilege in our homes and this responsibility to pass the light. You have the privilege to be the one to demonstrate what it means to let your light shine before your family and others so that they may see your good works and be left with no other choice but to "give glory to your Father who is in heaven" (Matthew 5:16 ESV). You get to model what it is to be a light-bearer, trusting in the Father, relying on the Spirit to help you moment by moment to share God's joy and hope. And we also get the privilege to show our kids what good repentance looks like when we fail to bear the light well.

Whatever you do, don't hide your light. You were made to shine.

When you think about being the light of Jesus in your home, think about the atmosphere you create by how you love Jesus openly and unashamedly. What specific things do you think God is calling you to do to create a joyful and God-honoring atmosphere in your home?

Speaking of light, what is your daytime routine like these days with your baby?

Even if He Does Not

If we are thrown into the blazing furnace,
the God we serve is able to deliver us
from it, and he will deliver us from Your
Majesty's hand. But even if he does
not . . . we will not serve your gods.
DANIEL 3:17–18 NIV

As moms, we likely will face situations where we need deliverance—whether it's a household financial crisis, a child's medical diagnosis, or a broken relationship beyond our ability to repair. The Israelites knew God as their deliverer. He was the mighty God who had brought them out of Egypt (Exodus 6:6), delivered them from attacks on the way to the promised land (Numbers 21:1–3), sent a line of deliverers when they repeatedly sinned in the age of the judges (Judges 3:9; 18:28), and made Himself known as deliverer to their beloved King David (Psalm 18:2; 40:1). It is natural, then, that when Shadrach, Meshach, and Abednego found themselves about to be thrown into a fiery furnace, they called out once again to that delivering God, known throughout their history. But what I find amazing about this passage is not their hope in His deliverance but their trust in Him *even if* He did not deliver them.

They knew that even though God was *able* to deliver them, whether or not He did was up to His sovereign will. They trusted that God was wise enough and good enough to decide their future. How about you? Will you profess His faithfulness whether He answers your prayers for deliverance with a yes, a no, or a wait?

Hard-Won Comfort

*He has delivered us from such a
deadly peril, and he will deliver us
again. On him we have set our hope
that he will continue to deliver us.*
2 CORINTHIANS 1:10 NIV

$\mathcal{P}$aul wrote to the church in Corinth his praise to the God of compassion "who comforts us in all our troubles, so that we can comfort those in any trouble with the comfort we ourselves receive from God" (2 Corinthians 1:4 NIV). It is a beautiful sentiment, but it is easy to gloss over how hard-won this comfort He offers is. Paul wrote, "We were under great pressure, far beyond our ability to endure, so that we despaired of life itself" (v. 8 NIV). This is comfort gained amid life's harshest difficulties. Notice: God did not *prevent* their hardships. He was *with* them *in the midst*.

Sometimes I don't want God the Deliverer. I want God the Preventer. I want the "Get out of jail free" card, not the "God will be with me in the midst of jail" card. But God often works this way. He didn't *prevent* the fiery furnace; He was *in* it. He didn't stop the tempest before it ever started for the disciples, but He was on the boat when the waves were crashing.

In some ways, motherhood feels like this line from Paul: "We were under great pressure, far beyond our ability." Maybe you feel that way some days too. How good to know that while God may not deliver us from that feeling, He is there in the midst of the pressure, in the midst of the difficulty. And He will use the hard-won comfort that you receive from Him in the midst of it to comfort someone else.

My Deliverer Is Coming!

"The Deliverer will come from Zion, he
will banish ungodliness from Jacob";
"and this will be my covenant with
them when I take away their sins."
ROMANS 11:26–27 ESV

Buried in the psyche of every Israelite was a steady belief that the Deliverer, the Messiah, was coming. That steadfast hope in a coming deliverer is grounded in the same Old Testament promises that today's verse in Romans references. These are verses such as "'The Redeemer will come to Zion, to those in Jacob who repent of their sins,' declares the LORD" (Isaiah 59:20 NIV). These words gave them courage in the dark years of exile.

Jesus was the fulfillment of that long-held expectation, but He wasn't the Deliverer that many expected. He didn't take up arms against their Roman foes in rebellion and re-establish a physical kingdom of Israel at that time. Jesus delivered the people of His day and our own from a bondage to sin and the suffering inherent in alienation from God. As you continue this journey of motherhood, there may be days that Jesus is not the Deliverer you are expecting—perhaps He doesn't obliterate colic, teething, or postpartum depression like you'd hoped. Those are the days we need to see what He *is* doing. Is He bringing people alongside to bear the burden? Is He comforting you with His Word? Is He working on your character? And we need to hope in the ultimate day of deliverance, which is coming, when every wrong will be made right, when every brokenness will be made whole, when every dark moment will be redeemed by His light.

Where have you experienced a "hard-won" comfort in Christ? Have you shared that comfort with others?

You've known your little one for almost half a year; how has your life changed?

Monthly Memories
and Milestones

What new skills has Baby mastered?

_____

_____

_____

_____

_____

_____

_____

Baby really likes it when . . .

_____

_____

_____

_____

_____

_____

_____

_____

One of the biggest world events since Baby was born has been . . .

One thing I had to learn (or relearn) since Baby came was . . .

One thing Baby has already changed in me is:

Your Six-Month-Old Developmental Guide

$\mathcal{H}$appy half-birthday, Baby! Can you believe it? Just six short months ago you were welcoming baby into your arms; now she's likely twice the size and filling your world with giggles, babbles, and joy! What milestones are likely in the month ahead? While every baby develops at his or her own rate, here is a list of common six-month developmental markers:

- Perceives objects across the room clearly (as eyesight nears adult levels)
- Starts moving objects between hands
- Uses a raking grasp (picking up objects with fingers open) that will become a pincer grasp (clasping with pointer finger and thumb) with time
- Bounces when held in a standing position
- Bears more weight on legs
- Babbles sounds, such as "ma" or "buh"
- Responds with sounds to you
- Recognizes familiar faces
- Rolls from front to back, and back to front
- Sits without support
- Recognizes his or her name

- Likes to look in a mirror
- Responds to emotions and communicates emotions with sounds
- Rocks back and forth on hands and knees
- Begins to "scoot" backward

Because all babies develop at their own rate, when should you be concerned and talk to a doctor? If your baby is not responding to affection, not making sounds or any happy sounds, you should talk to your pediatrician. If Baby is unable to roll, doesn't attempt to reach, or is not gaining weight, discuss these issues with the doctor familiar with your child's growth and developmental curve.

Speaking of milestones, this is the month when most babies begin sampling solids. But it's good not to go just by age but rather look for signs of developmental readiness. For instance, does Baby show interest in food as it goes to your mouth or open her mouth when food is nearby? Does Baby sit up without support, and has her birth weight doubled? If so, it might be time to break out the bibs. While experts used to recommend introducing foods in a certain order, starting with an iron-fortified cereal grain like finely ground oats, today's experts say there is no particular right order and instead suggest starting with fresh foods. They also suggest introducing new foods one at a time, waiting several days to a week for the introduction of the next food item, so that you can watch for signs of food allergies or reactions.

Our Shield

*But you, LORD, are a shield around me,
my glory, the One who lifts my head high.*
PSALM 3:3 NIV

$\mathcal{V}$igilance—that's the name of the game as Baby begins to be more mobile. One minute she's happily playing on the mat, the next she's rolled her way over to the television set and is yanking on cords. With your baby rapidly changing from stationary to more mobile, anxiety can creep in. What dangers should you anticipate?

While we have a responsibility to think ahead, we also can't foresee or prevent every danger. And in the midst of this need comes the truth that our God is a shield and a defending warrior. In ancient Israel, there were two types of shields often used (2 Chronicles 23:9). One was a smaller shield that could be held by a warrior. It was light and maneuverable. The other, the kind David likely had in mind, was enormous—a concave, rectangular shape, often held by a special defender, a shield-bearer like Goliath had when he fought young David (1 Samuel 17:41). This warrior shielded another soldier with a full-bodied and robust defense.

David would certainly have known God as this kind of defender: the One who could protect him from a nine-foot giant, the thrusts of a mad king's spears, and later, his pursuing army. God even protected David from himself (1 Samuel 25:33). David knew God as this kind of defense, the One who lifted his head when he felt dejected. Mama, whatever today's struggles, remember God encircles you. As we lift our faces to behold His wonder, as we realize that He is where our glory and identity lie, we can face any circumstance with confidence.

Our God Is a Mighty Warrior

The LORD is my strength and song, and
He has become my salvation; He is my
God, and I will praise Him; . . . The LORD
is a man of war; the LORD is His name.

EXODUS 15:2–3

$\mathcal{G}$ rowing up with two older brothers, I always had confidence that if anyone wanted to mess with me, they'd have to get through my brothers first. Knowing you have someone who has your back gives you courage. In the book of Exodus, the Israelites were against a wall. The Red Sea was before them, and chariots were behind them. They were completely out of resources, time, and hope—that's the moment their God, the warrior, flexed His arm.

Here, God was "a man of war" who would not tolerate an enemy tormenting His people. He waged war with those who waged war against them. This hero, God, hurled chariots into the sea (v. 4), flared His nostrils and made the seas writhe and stand in a heap and congeal (v. 8). And the reputation of this mighty warrior God now went before the people of Israel and made their enemies quake—this one true God fighting for the Israelites.

As the Israelites faced yet another unknown while entering the land, they needed to know their warrior God went before them. How about you? What unknowns are stressing you out? Starting solids? Possible food allergies? Baby's growing mobility and all the hazards she can get into? Changing dynamics with an older sibling? Breakdowns in relationships or financial pressures? Know that your warrior God goes before you.

When God Calls a Coward "Warrior"

When the angel of the LORD appeared to Gideon, he said, "The LORD is with you, mighty warrior."
JUDGES 6:12 NIV

Maybe you heard your baby's 5:00 a.m. wake-up cry and pulled the covers up over your head. Or maybe your toddler's tantrum has you hiding in the bathroom. Every mom faces moments of overload—moments where she'd rather hide than be the hero. And sometimes those are the exact moments when God shows up and calls us by a name that we don't deserve. He calls us daring when we are dodging; He calls us warrior when we are weary; He calls us brave when we are baffled; He calls us overcomers when we are overcome.

That's what God did here for Gideon. The angel of the Lord found Gideon threshing wheat in a winepress. Usually, wheat would be threshed in open places, where the wind could carry the chaff away. But Gideon was cowering. He was terrified of the Midianites stealing his harvest. Israel had forgotten their God, the "man of war" who'd hurled Pharaoh's chariots into the sea and brought the walls of Jericho tumbling (Exodus 15:3; Joshua 6:20). Instead, Gideon was pulling up the covers. But God didn't leave Gideon; He called him to action. He called this reluctant hero. God then downsized his army and defeated the mighty Midianites with a trumpet blast and empty jars. God showed Gideon, "I've got this. I'm the hero these people need." Like Gideon, all we need to do is show up and let God be the hero our story needs.

Write a prayer that your baby will grow into an adult of courage undergirded by the great strength of our warrior God.

Your little one is half a year old! What has been your favorite part of mothering him or her?

God of Forgiveness

Let the wicked forsake his way, and
the unrighteous man his thoughts; let
him return to the LORD, that he may
have compassion on him, and to our
God, for he will abundantly pardon.
ISAIAH 55:7 ESV

$\mathcal{M}$om guilt—it's real. Maybe you've never heard of it. Maybe you can't shake it. But for many moms, that feeling of not being enough or doing enough is something she battles constantly.

Here's the good news. We serve a forgiving God. He's big enough to help us when the guilt is legitimate and big enough to calm our fears when the guilt is false.

When the guilt is real, when we've failed, we need to hear Nehemiah's words: "You are a God of forgiveness, gracious and compassionate, slow to anger and abounding in lovingkindness" (9:17 NASB 1995). We need to remember that gracious and forgiving are key attributes of God.

But what if the feelings are based in unreasonable expectations? What about the mom who feels guilty for not holding her baby all the time? Or who worries that her older child will be scarred for life because Mom spends so much time nursing the new baby? God speaks into false guilt as well. John wrote, "If our hearts condemn us, we know that God is greater than our hearts, and he knows everything" (1 John 3:19–20 NIV).

God is greater than our hearts. Ask Him to shine the truth into your heart and show you when you are heaping guilt on yourself that shouldn't be there. Wherever you are today, know that our forgiving God can cleanse you of guilt, both real and false.

Forgive and Forget

For as high as the heavens are above
the earth, so great is his love for those
who fear him; as far as the east is
from the west, so far has he removed
our transgressions from us.

PSALM 103:11–12 NIV

We rented an older house once where the kitchen sink constantly backed up. We finally called the landlord, and he sent a repairman. Inside those pipes, years of grease and grime had built up and there was hardly room for the water to drain. Relationships are like that. As a mom, you will need to forgive your kids, your spouse, even yourself, time and again. If you don't, the muck in the pipes of everyday life is going to build up to the point that nothing runs smoothly. When God forgives us, He casts our sin as far as the east is from the west. We can't even fathom that distance. And He calls us to do the same.

For us, it also means that if we have repented of our sins, we need not fear drawing close to God. He has completely forgiven us. As Isaiah 43:25 says, "I, even I, am he who blots out your transgressions, for my own sake, and remembers your sins no more" (NIV). And Romans 8:1 reminds us that there is now no condemnation for those who are in Christ. Because Christ's sacrifice is once and for all, we need not fear God holding us to account for the same sin again (see Hebrews 10). Like King Hezekiah, we can praise God, saying, "You have put all my sins behind your back" (Isaiah 38:17 NIV). Let these thoughts draw you closer to God and buoy your heart today in grateful praise.

Called to Forgive

*"Be angry, and do not sin": do not let
the sun go down on your wrath.*
EPHESIANS 4:26

$\mathcal{D}$id you know that, on average, babies deprive their parents of the equivalent of forty-four days of sleep in their first year?[1] If your nights are still being punctuated by feedings or if Baby thinks 5:00 a.m. is a great time to start the day, chances are you may find yourself more irritable and emotional as the interrupted sleep takes its toll on your body. And whether you've gone back to work or are staying home, with more demands and less personal time, it's not surprising that you find yourself falling into conflict.

The Bible gives us such great practical wisdom in navigating conflict. For example, Paul instructed us to keep short accounts when it comes to sin. He told us not to "let the sun go down" on our wrath. We are to seek forgiveness, reconciliation, and restoration quickly so that our relationships don't deteriorate. God calls us to "bear with each other and forgive one another. . . . Forgive as the Lord forgave you" (Colossians 3:13 NIV). Bearing with one another is not taking offense at the slightest grievance. Christ's forgiveness of us animates our forgiveness of others. His forgiveness was costly, moving into our deep need even before we were able to repent. Likewise, He may call you to take the initiative in reconciliation, opening a pathway for repentance by the offer of grace. Moms, this is hard—too hard for us outside the Spirit's enabling work. But as we cry out for strength, God supplies our need, animating us with the power to forgive.

Mothers—like every other human on the planet—are going to mess up. What do you think your child will learn from you if you are willing to ask forgiveness when your sins and failures affect him or her? How can these moments become opportunities one day to point your son or daughter to Jesus?

Planes, trains, and automobiles—oh the places your little one will go! Have you taken any major trips yet with Baby, or do you have something planned? What distant places are you excited to share with your son or daughter one day?

Strength Under Control

Put your sword in its place. . . . do you think that I cannot now pray to My Father, and He will provide Me with more than twelve legions of angels?
MATTHEW 26:52–53

A recent study found that babies as young as fifteen months old remembered an adult who got angry, and the babies altered their behavior to avoid being a target. Though our little ones are small, our behavior profoundly affects them.[1]

In the New Testament, the Greek word *praus* is sometimes translated "meekness" and "gentleness." It literally means "strength under control." It was often associated with the training of a war horse. That horse had to have incredible discipline to follow orders and maintain calmness in the noise and chaos of battle. *Praus* is used twice in the New Testament to describe Jesus. First, in Matthew 11:29 where Jesus described Himself as "gentle and lowly," and second, in Matthew 21:5, referencing how the king will come: meek and riding a donkey. Jesus exemplified this character of strength under control, especially during His arrest.

As Roman soldiers with clubs and swords came in the night, Peter sliced off the ear of one of the high priest's servants (John 18:10). Jesus reminded Peter that He had legions of angels at His disposal. The power of the universe was at Jesus' fingertips, but He exercised strength under control. Mama, your household is sometimes going to feel like the chaos of a battlefield. It's easy to let tempers flare, to shout to be heard. But God calls us to a different kind of power: the gentleness and meekness of Jesus, whose strength was harnessed by God for the purposes of God.

Meekness: The Power to Wait

Look, this day your eyes have seen that the LORD delivered you today into my hand in the cave, and someone urged me to kill you. But my eye spared you.

1 SAMUEL 24:10

Meekness is not a quality valued today. We live in a world where the loudest, the strongest, and the smartest are prized for their brass. He or she who gets the last word, the final point, or the edge up is the one our culture tends to admire. God calls us to be different.

David is a beautiful model of this different way. Even though Saul was pursuing David with three thousand men at En Gedi, even though God had already promised the throne to David, even though David had caught Saul defenseless, David did not trust in his own might but in God's timing and justice. He left the matter to God. What a moment of meekness!

Moms, where is God asking you to wait on His timing? Perhaps, you are waiting on Baby to accept solids, waiting for a work-from-home position, or waiting on the timing of a move. Where is He stretching you to trust His good heart for you in the unknown? The psalms show how David soaked in the truths of God's character: "The LORD is my light and my salvation; whom shall I fear?" or "The LORD is my rock and my fortress and my deliverer; my God, my strength, in whom I will trust" (Psalm 27:1; 18:2). Like David, ask God to help you meditate today on His strength. And let that give you the courage to wait on Him, exercising the power of meekness—strength under control.

The Earth's Heirs

Blessed are the meek, for they
shall inherit the earth.

MATTHEW 5:5

*H*ave you ever met a truly meek person? If you have, you know they can have an impermeable character. It is as if the world's worst simply cannot touch them. When Jesus talks about turning the other cheek or offering a second cloak when the first is taken, He is describing the strength of the meek. This isn't cowardice. This is the strength of God displayed in forbearance. And when evil man can't touch someone's inner spirit, can't dampen the beauty of someone's trust in Jesus, there is a great sense that person has already inherited the earth. Paul wrote, "All things are yours . . . all are yours, and you are of Christ, and Christ is of God" (1 Corinthians 3:21–23 NIV).

Of course, there is also a sense in which the inheritance of the meek is a future inheritance. Those who have trusted in God to bring justice await the day when that justice will come. The faithful who gave up worldly possessions, who suffered persecutions, who chose to be pilgrims because they awaited a better country, as Hebrews 11 lists, await the abundance of their heavenly reward. Moms, we don't know what God may ask us to walk through as we raise our children. The years to come may hold peace or war, feast or famine, calm or disaster, at home or abroad, but we do know a kingdom hope that can give us grace to live with the unflappable peace of the meek.

How does the definition of gentleness or meekness as strength under control appeal to you? How is it difficult for you?

Strength under control—what a beautiful thing to teach our children! Why do you think it's important to raise kids to understand that true strength is strength submitted to God?

The Generosity of God

Oh, how abundant is your goodness, which you have stored up for those who fear you and worked for those who take refuge in you, in the sight of the children of mankind!
PSALM 31:19 ESV

Growing up near the beach, one of my favorite childhood activities was digging for coquina shells in the sand with my mom. Recently, I got to share this joy with my sons on Fort Myers Beach. We laid out these tiny bivalves, scarcely bigger than a fingernail, making a breathtaking mosaic of every color of the sunset.

Why do I mention this? The world at our fingertips is a catalog of God's overflowing generosity. Every square inch of creation, from the skies above with their ten thousand species of birds to the waves below with the one million species of sea animals to that handful of sand with its ten thousand individual grains, shouts His generosity. As a mom, one of your joyful jobs will be pointing out God's generosity in creation to your children like my mom did for me and as I have the privilege of doing for my kids. We get to show them that God lavished us with the variety of His creation—and that He longs to lavish His goodness on us. David imagined God with a storehouse, waiting to rain down goodness on us at the proper time. God's heart is generous: He gives wisdom (James 1:5), He supplies our needs (Philippians 4:19), He gives joy (John 16:23–24), and best of all, He gave His Son (John 3:16). In Him, we have every spiritual blessing, grace upon grace, salvation, eternity, adoption by God, and relationship with the Father. May our hearts revel in this generous God, and may we teach our children to do the same!

A Serpent or a Fish?

Or what man is there among you who, if his son asks for bread, will give him a stone? Or if he asks for a fish, will he give him a serpent?
MATTHEW 7:9–10

Recently my eleven-year-old son asked for an end-of-school water party. His boyish imagination came alive with visions of water guns and water balloons, forts, friends, and splashy warfare. As parents with finite resources, even though our hearts are full of goodness, we can't give our children some things: trips around the world, acres of land, and a menagerie of pets. So when I could make my son's dreams for an epic water fight come alive, this was deep joy. Five hundred water balloons later, my son gave the "atta girl" a mom's heart needs: "Mom, that water fight was epic!"

Guess what? God's heart toward us is epic. He longs to lavish on us every spiritual blessing in Christ (Ephesians 1:3). "Ask, and it will be given to you; seek, and you will find; knock, and it will be opened to you" (Matthew 7:7). He shows us the extent of that love through His most lavish gift of all: His Son. And then, the apostle Paul reminded us, "He who did not spare His own Son, but delivered Him up for us all, how shall He not with Him also freely give us all things?" (Romans 8:32). If my heart longs to give good gifts to my children, imagine God's. Let us then go boldly and ask for the grace we need, trusting that whatever God answers, His generosity is always epic.

Overflowing Generosity

*In a great trial of affliction the abundance
of their joy and their deep poverty
abounded in the riches of their liberality.*

2 CORINTHIANS 8:2

God doesn't give stingily or grudgingly. He isn't working on a budget, cutting corners, or giving just the bare minimum. He gives abundantly, lavishly, with an overflowing generosity. And sometimes that generosity costs Him deeply, yet He gives with joy. What a beautiful model for us!

I love how the church in Macedonia that Paul was writing about in today's verse internalized the generosity of God and then followed His example. Despite "great trial of affliction," their generosity "abounded." It overflowed from the "abundance of their joy." They gave "beyond their ability" and "freely." They were able to do this because they "first gave themselves to the Lord" (2 Corinthians 8:5). You see, when our giving is first a gift to the Lord, then our thankfulness to the Father overflows in generosity to others.

Where is God calling you to be generous today? Is it with your time, your attention, your talents, your finances? Maybe He is simply calling you to lavish the fullness of your love on your little one as you meet those very basic needs for love, attention, and care. Perhaps the generosity He is calling you to requires a sacrifice of the things you crave most: comfort or quiet or credit. But whatever He is calling you to give, let your love for Jesus fuel the giving. Let your gratitude to Him overflow in goodness toward others. This is worship.

Little one, I want to tell you about how God has been generous with me . . .

What has been your hardest adjustment since Baby's arrival?

Monthly Memories
and Milestones

Baby's first foods were . . .

_____

_____

_____

_____

_____

_____

Baby showed what he thought about those first foods by . . .

_____

_____

_____

_____

_____

_____

_____

One thing I often find myself praying for Baby is . . .

How and when did Baby begin to master sitting up?

Other moments or milestones from this month:

Your Seven-Month-Old Developmental Guide

*Y*ou've probably perfected a few moves by now—like the mama sway and the mama bounce—to soothe your little one, but soon your baby will be showing off some moves of his own. Did you have any idea there were so many types of crawls: the army crawl, the backward crawl, the sitting scoot, the crab scoot (with one leg extended in the air), or the crawling scoot? Like everything else, your child will develop on his own timetable. And however he crawls, your life will be changing a lot as your little one becomes more mobile.

Speaking of life changing, as your baby begins to eat more table food, you may find your own body changing: your menstrual cycle may return if you are breastfeeding less, and with it your ability to conceive again. Make sure you and your spouse are prayerfully on the same page as these changes occur. If you've been breastfeeding and those feedings are becoming less frequent either now or in the months to come, be aware that your hormones and mood may also change. Some women may experience postpartum symptoms that coincide with the decrease in breastfeeding frequency and the corresponding hormonal changes. Be aware of this and make sure to talk to someone you trust and your doctor if you are finding yourself emotionally off-balance. Postpartum depression and anxiety are both very real; take them seriously, and if you ever feel a desire to hurt yourself or your baby, dial 911.

And speaking of emergencies, as your little one becomes more mobile, injuries are more likely to happen. Make sure you babyproof ahead of the milestones since you never know when those milestones will happen. Also keep your pediatrician's phone number handy, especially for anyone who might be watching baby.

Other milestones you should watch for this month include

- Responds to talking by making sounds
- Recognizes basic words like "cup," "ball," or "bed"
- Reacts to name
- Makes noises based on emotions: happy, sad, frustrated, etc.
- Recognizes familiar faces
- Reacts to strangers by seeking solace in the familiar
- Bears more weight on legs
- Rolls from front to back or back to front
- Sits without support
- Begins to crawl or shows interest in moving
- Passes object from one hand to the other

Jesus as Our Friend

No longer do I call you servants . .
. but I have called you friends.
JOHN 15:15

My first year of motherhood was particularly disorienting because the landscape of my friendships changed so much. After maternity leave, I went back to work, but remotely. Female friends married and moved away; work friends were now virtual. In some ways, that first year of motherhood was a lonely time, where I had to work to forge new friendships and hold on to old ones. Maybe you are experiencing this now, maybe not. But wherever you are, it's helpful to remember that Jesus calls us friends. He could have called us servant, but instead He chose friend.

Think about how different these two terms are. A servant helps because he is ordered to do so. A friend helps because he loves his friend. A servant may bring food to the table, but he certainly doesn't stay to fellowship. A servant is obliged, a friend is free. A servant cannot speak freely; a friend is invited to speak his mind. A servant comes when he is bid; a friend is welcome to call whenever he wants.

By calling us friends, Jesus invites us to intimacy, to fellowship, to speak freely, to enjoy the spontaneity of real relationship. No matter what the landscape of your friendships looks like since having Baby, Jesus invites you into the comfort and joy of the best friendship you could possibly know. He is a friend who is closer than a brother—a friend who never leaves our side.

Cultivating Friendship
with God

The friendship of the LORD is for
those who fear him, and he makes
known to them his covenant.
PSALM 25:14 ESV

*W*hen I had my first son, those early months with a newborn were so draining; I hardly had the time for friends. But as he grew and the landscape of my friendships changed, I worked on cultivating new friendships with other moms. I worked at it. I invited mommy friends for playdates (often the playdates were at least as much for us as for the babies). Sometimes only a few shreds of real conversation happened as babies and toddlers demanded our attention. But we kept working at it because we needed it.

Cultivating friendships takes work. And it is not surprising that our friendship with God grows better with effort. There are two people in the Old Testament whom God specifically called "friend": Abraham and Moses (2 Chronicles 20:7; Isaiah 41:8). Abraham left everything familiar to follow God. He walked with God, listened to Him, and believed Him. Of Moses it is said, "The LORD would speak to Moses face to face, as one speaks to a friend" (Exodus 33:11 NIV). Both men modeled the principle taught in Scripture: "Draw near to God and He will draw near to you" (James 4:8). Friendship also meant receiving correction: "Wounds from a friend can be trusted, but an enemy multiplies kisses" (Proverbs 27:6 NIV). Whatever season of friendship you're in, you can cultivate friendship with God by drawing near to Him. As you do, you'll be learning to be a better friend in your everyday world.

The Ultimate Act of Friendship

Greater love has no one than this: to lay down one's life for one's friends. You are my friends if you do what I command.
JOHN 15:13–14 NIV

Many women struggle with friendship during this time in their lives. It's easy to default to inaction or self-pity, but God offers us a beautiful secret to deeper friendship: laying down our lives.

There is no greater love than laying down one's life for one's friends. Jesus modeled for us how to show friendship to others. Few of us will be called to lay our lives down in the physical sense of that word, but all of us are called to sacrifice regularly to love others. In fact, it is often in sacrifice that real friendship blooms.

Are you out of step with friends? Perhaps the joy of life with Baby makes it harder for your single friend or the one struggling with infertility. Can you ask your husband or a babysitter to watch Baby so you can get out on your own? Lay down your life by focusing your attention and your conversation on your friend for the evening. You can chat about Baby's progress with solids some other time.

Maybe you have a friend struggling in her marriage—can you lay down your life by watching her toddler so she can have a night out with her spouse? Or perhaps God will call you to give the money you were saving for a nice vacation to help a friend's dream of adoption come true. You can bemoan a lack of friendship, or you can be the friend you wish you had. Jesus shows us the most excellent way.

How can you cultivate deeper friendships during this new season of life?

Which of your friends has loved on your baby and on you during these months of welcoming your new little one into the world?

A Ready Counselor

*I bless the LORD who gives me counsel;
in the night also my heart instructs me.*
PSALM 16:7 ESV

 A s the parent of an infant, you'll find people constantly offer unsolicited advice. Whether singing the praises of homemade pureed, organic vegetables or lauding the freedom of co-sleeping, they'll likely offer plenty of counsel. But not all the advice will be right for you. Wouldn't it be nice if there were someone who completely and intimately knew your circumstances, your child's personality, your strengths and your weaknesses, the future and the past, and could guide you perfectly?

Well, too often we fail to realize that there is. While the Bible doesn't give us instructions on the nitty-gritty details of every aspect of parenting, God wants us to come to Him with even the small decisions that burden our minds. In this passage, the psalmist blessed the Lord as the one who counseled him and instructed his heart even at night. Have you ever felt so burdened about a decision at night and prayed about it only to wake up with a new sense of clarity? That isn't a coincidence. That is an answered prayer. Our job is to ask God in prayer; as James wrote, "If any of you lacks wisdom, let him ask of God, who gives to all liberally and without reproach, and it will be given to him" (James 1:5). God is rich in counsel and wisdom, but He is not pushy. He longs to guide us but wants us to seek Him. Will you come to Him today?

An Ever-Present Counselor

Your Seven-Month-Old,
Week Two Theme:
Counselor

*However, when He, the Spirit of truth, has
come, He will guide you into all truth; for
He will not speak on His own authority,
but whatever He hears He will speak;
and He will tell you things to come.*

JOHN 16:13

$\mathcal{I}$ can't imagine the emotion of the last few weeks of Jesus' ministry with His disciples. The disciples had spent every waking moment in Jesus' presence; they knew an intimacy and fellowship like no other. And now it was time to say goodbye. Jesus knew the horror and shock that the crucifixion would be to their senses. He knew how abandoned and alone they would feel. He knew the persecution that was coming. What possible comfort could He offer?

Jesus offered the best comfort imaginable. He offered the comfort and counsel of the Holy Spirit. He offered a friendship that would be with each of them, whether in prison cells, before tyrants, or on deserted islands. This Spirit of truth would guide them and teach them (John 14:26). The Spirit is also a Spirit of power (Acts 1:8). The Spirit is an intercessor (Romans 8:26–27). The Spirit unifies us (1 Corinthians 12:13), equips us (1 Corinthians 12:8–11), produces fruit in us (Galatians 5:22), sends us (Acts 13:2), stops us (Acts 16:6–7), and frees us (2 Corinthians 3:17). Mamas, Jesus also offers that indescribable parting gift to us! Whatever your fears about the next stage of parenting, whatever worries you are facing balancing Baby's needs and others' needs, whatever need you have, you have a ready counselor!

An Apt Counsel

And we urge you, brothers, admonish
the idle, encourage the fainthearted, help
the weak, be patient with them all.
1 THESSALONIANS 5:14 ESV

While not all of us are called to be professional counselors, we should be equipped to offer godly counsel by knowing God's Word and walking in the Spirit. In Thessalonians, Paul encouraged believers to pay attention to the needs of those around them so they would be able to discern others' needs and respond appropriately: warning the idle, encouraging the fainthearted, and helping the weak. The need dictated the response.

In Proverbs, Solomon compared this ability to give an apt word of counsel to "apples of gold in settings of silver" (Proverbs 25:11). This is how beautiful an apt word is at an apt time. It is something of exceeding beauty; and this is something we can offer as we look and listen to the needs of others and live in line with the Spirit. The prophet Isaiah wrote, "The LORD God has given me the tongue of those who are taught, that I may know how to sustain with a word him who is weary" (Isaiah 50:4 ESV). We can pray that God will give us both the ear and the tongue of those who are taught, that we might be His instruments to offer sustaining power to the weary and to truly listen. These are gifts so needed today. Whether it's the mom in your daughter's play group who is going through a difficult season, a colleague at work, or your own spouse—God can use you to be His eyes, ears, and voice to the people around you.

What good counsel have you received from a parent or mentor that you would like to pass on to your child?

When you are grown, my dear one, I hope you will remember . . .

Our Keeper

*He will not allow your foot to be moved;
He who keeps you will not slumber. Behold,
He who keeps Israel shall neither slumber
nor sleep. The Lord is your keeper.*
PSALM 121:3–5

During the interrupted nights of mothering an infant, it's comforting to know that God neither slumbers nor sleeps. He's awake too! Here in this passage, though, the emphasis is on God as our keeper or protector. This psalm begins with the lines "I will lift up my eyes to the hills—from whence comes my help?" (Psalm 121:1). These are not picturesque, postcard-perfect hills. In this time, hills were associated with enemies and bandits (Numbers 23:7; Judges 6:2), wild animals (1 Samuel 26:20; 1 Chronicles 12:8), places where one could slip and fall (Jeremiah 13:16), and places where pagan people worshiped (Deuteronomy 12:2; Hosea 4:13). His point was God has the power to protect us from danger both physical and spiritual on the journey.

In today's psalm, the line "the Lord is your keeper" is at the exact midpoint, a Hebrew poetic device used to highlight the most important point. There are exactly fifteen Hebrew syllables preceding it and exactly fifteen Hebrew syllables following it. The words remind us of the Aaronic blessing: "The Lord bless you and keep you; the Lord make His face shine upon you, and be gracious to you; the Lord lift up His countenance upon you, and give you peace" (Numbers 6:24–26). What a comfort to remember with the psalmist that no matter the dangers that lie in life's journey, the Lord will be our keeper.

Baby Gates and God's Hedges

You, O LORD, will keep them; You will preserve him from this generation forever.
PSALM 12:7 NASB 1995

Babyproofing—as your little one begins to be mobile, protecting him is top of mind. It is not that we want to limit our children's freedom. Rather, our love motivates our desire to protect. David knew what it was like to keep his flock from harm. And as one hunted by Saul, it is only natural that David would turn to God as his keeper.

We find the word *keeper* translated from three different Hebrew words. *Tsaphan* means "to hide or cover." This is the word David used in Psalm 31 when he wrote, "How great is Your goodness, which You have stored up [*tsaphan*] for those who fear You. . . . You hide them in the secret place of Your presence from the conspiracies of man; You keep [*tsaphan*] them secretly in a shelter from the strife of tongues" (vv. 19–20 NASB 1995). God's keeping is a hiding or a cover. Two other verbs translate as "to keep," which we see in today's passage in Psalm 12. These are the words *natsar*, which means "to guard with fidelity," and *shamar*, which means "to surround as a means of protection." In Psalm 12:7, David wrote, "You, O LORD, will keep [*shamar*] them; You will preserve [*natsar*] him from this generation forever" (NASB 1995).

Whether we realize it or not, whether we feel it or not, God is continually keeping us. That doesn't mean no harm will befall us, but it does mean He will preserve our spirits through it.

My Brother's Keeper

Then the LORD said to Cain, "Where is
Abel your brother?" He said, "I do not
know. Am I my brother's keeper?"
GENESIS 4:9

In the tragic account of the world's first murder, God asked Cain a simple question. "Where is your brother?" He responded with a defiant question: "Am I my brother's keeper?" His question echoes down through the ages. Does God want us to be our brother's keeper? The Bible seems clear on this. The apostle John wrote, "If someone says, 'I love God,' and hates his brother, he is a liar; for he who does not love his brother whom he has seen, how can he love God whom he has not seen?" (1 John 4:20). We have a responsibility to love our neighbor, whoever that may be.

How much further that responsibility goes, though, when it comes to our own offspring! We have a responsibility to nurture and discipline (Ephesians 6:4), to train (Proverbs 22:6), to provide for (1 Timothy 5:8), and to care for the emotional health of our children (Colossians 3:21). We are to be our child's keeper, tenderly nurturing them to know they are loved by us and by the Father. We have been entrusted with the most precious of trusts—the tending of a human soul. That doesn't mean the salvation of our children depends on us. God is sovereign over salvation. But it does mean that we plant seeds, we water them, and we wait on God for the growth we so long to see (1 Corinthians 3:6). Mamas, I can't say this enough—you have a high and holy calling. This precious gift that rolls and reaches, stretches and yawns before your eyes is a sacred trust you've been given. Keep that trust well. And remember your calling is so important.

Where can you look back and see God's keeping hand in your life? Where have you misjudged His boundaries or limitations in your life when they were lovingly meant for your keeping?

What does babyproofing look like in your house? Is your baby getting into things he shouldn't?

Community at the Heart of God

Heaven was opened, and he saw the Spirit of God descending like a dove and alighting on him. And a voice from heaven said, "This is my Son, whom I love; with him I am well pleased."

MATTHEW 3:16–17 NIV

$\mathcal{S}$ ometimes the curtains are pulled back, and we inadvertently catch a glimpse of deep relationship: an elderly couple clasping wrinkled hands together at a restaurant, the father lovingly kissing away his daughter's tears on the playground, or a big brother taking a little brother by the hand as they cross the street. The baptism of Jesus is one such moment.

At the baptism of Jesus we see the approval of God voiced from heaven, the delight of the Son in glorifying His Father, and the descent of the Spirit of God bringing glory to the Son, which in turn brings glory to the Father. There is in this moment a kind of dance of glory-giving and receiving, of pleasure and approval that is a beauty to behold. In John 17:24, Jesus prayed, "Father, I desire that they also whom You gave Me may be with Me where I am, that they may behold My glory which You have given Me; for You loved Me before the foundation of the world." God has pulled back the curtains to give us a glimpse of relationship in its perfection—and then invites us into the joy. Not only for us individually, but He beckons us to let this glimpse of deep fellowship, of giving and receiving, of honoring and bringing honor, give us a vision for our families.

What the Communal God Means for Us

*Go therefore and make disciples
of all the nations, baptizing them
in the name of the Father and of
the Son and of the Holy Spirit.*

MATTHEW 28:19

$\mathcal{A}$s we talked about in the last devotion, at the heart of God is relationship. Our God is not a lonely God but a God who exists in perpetual, perfect community. So when God gave instructions in today's verse for the expansion of His community, it is meaningful that He said to baptize people in the name of the Father, Son, and Holy Spirit. Not only are we called into the communal heart of the Trinity, but we are called to be a part of a community, the body of believers called the church. God never designed us to do the Christian life alone. This goes completely against the grain of modern thinking: that religion is a private affair. It flies in the face of our cultural individualism that says we don't need anyone but ourselves.

Mamas, are you attached to a local body of believers? Are you enjoying the community God made you to enjoy, giving to that community and inviting others into that community in the same way that God invited you into the fellowship of Father, Son, and Holy Spirit? It's so important for us and our children to grow in the context of a body of believers. They need to see you seeking out the fellowship, prayer, and counsel of believers. We aren't meant to do life alone.

One Another

A new commandment I give to you, that you love one another; as I have loved you, that you also love one another.
JOHN 13:34

How does community help us grow? It only takes a cursory look at the New Testament to see how often the writers used the phrase "one another." We are called to love (John 13:34—and sixteen other times), honor (Romans 12:10), accept (Romans 15:7), admonish (Romans 15:14), care for (1 Corinthians 12:25), serve (Galatians 5:13), forgive (Ephesians 4:2, 32), submit to (Ephesians 5:21), bear with (Colossians 3:13), teach (Colossians 3:16), comfort (1 Thessalonians 4:18), encourage (1 Thessalonians 5:11), exhort (Hebrews 3:13), pray for (James 5:16), and confess our faults all to "one another" (James 5:16). And that's just part of the list! Undoubtedly, our growth as Christians is to happen in this "one another" context.

Our children need us to be a part of Christian community. For it is this community that holds us accountable. It is this community where they will see Christ in others. It is in community where they will see you pray and receive prayer, serve and be served. All these aspects of community will ignite your spiritual growth as well as theirs. It will fuel your family's spiritual lives. Don't miss out or neglect all that God intends for you and your children through Christian community. As our lives blaze together, they make a greater witness to the world than our lives could apart.

Are you living a connected life with your church community? Who has God blessed you with through your church?

Write a prayer for your baby to grow up within the blessings of a vibrant body of believers, enjoying the benefits and responsibilities of life within a local, God-honoring church.

Monthly Memories and Milestones

I see a lot of resemblance in Baby to . . .

_____

_____

_____

_____

_____

Baby's favorite toys right now are . . .

_____

_____

_____

_____

_____

_____

_____

One special holiday we celebrated recently with Baby was . . .

My favorite thing to do with Baby right now is . . .

Baby's grandparents have enjoyed seeing Baby . . .

Your Eight-Month-Old Developmental Guide

"B a-ba-ba-ba, da-da-da" are probably sounds you are hearing a lot at your house these days. Your little one is likely enjoying exploring his or her vocal range and the wonderful sounds those lips and tongue can create. One of the most important things you can do for that sponge-like brain is to expose her to lots of words. Talk to your baby; narrate your day's activities, and read, read, read. Though some of these things may make you feel silly, the more words and sounds you expose her to at this point, the more her brain will develop. Let her hear music as well and explore the world through her ears.

While we are talking about exploring, don't be discouraged if your baby is not crawling yet. As you've heard many times before now, babies will develop according to their own timetables. If your child is not yet trying to push up, however, you can encourage him with lots of tummy time and by putting toys just out of reach.

Speaking of milestones and brain development, one of the best things you can do to help him reach baby goals is to allow him plenty of sleep. At this stage, your infant needs between fourteen to sixteen hours of sleep, and as counterintuitive as it may seem, sleep is prime time for brain development and skill consolidation. Most likely your baby will be taking two good naps (morning and afternoon) by now. If he is having trouble sleeping through the night, see if the final nap is lasting too long or if bedtime is too late. Believe it or not, if Baby has passed from sleepy to hyperstimulated, it may affect his ability to stay asleep. Sometimes moving bedtime earlier can help your infant fall asleep and stay asleep. Experiment with dropping a third short catnap or an earlier bedtime if night-wakings are still frequent.

Here are more milestones to watch for this month:

- Sits without support
- Rocks back and forth on knees
- Scoots backward or starts to crawl
- Bangs toys together
- Focuses on objects across the room
- Puts more weight on legs and bounces in standing position
- Uses raking grasp or develops pincer grasp
- Pulls up to standing position using support
- Recognizes familiar faces and reacts to strangers
- Babbles with consonant sounds or by stringing vowels together
- Likes to look in a mirror
- Reacts to name
- Understands basic cause and effect
- Responds when spoken to
- Shows emotions with sounds or face

Sacrificial Love

Abraham answered [to Isaac], "God
himself will provide the lamb for
the burnt offering, my son." And the
two of them went on together.
GENESIS 22:8 NIV

The story of Isaac has always moved me. But since becoming a parent, it is almost too painful to read. As the reader, we know from the outset that this is a test. In fact, in the very first line, it says, "After these things God tested Abraham" (Genesis 22:1 ESV). But from the text, there is no indication that Abraham knew it was a test. He climbed that mountain, gathered that wood, built an altar, bound his son, and took the knife, all without knowing the outcome of the story.

I knew from the time I was a little girl that I wanted to be a mommy when I grew up. I knew it before I knew I wanted to be a writer and before I knew what my taste in music would be. But I waited a long time before that dream came true. Perhaps that's why my sympathy with Abraham, who waited his whole life for fatherhood, is so high. And then to finally receive the promised gift only to be asked to relinquish it . . . well, it all seems so hard.

But I think God wants us to feel the depth of this sacrifice because He knew Abraham would not have to make it. But God would: "For God so loved the world"—that's you and me—"that He gave His only begotten Son" (John 3:16). Let us feel all the emotions alongside Abraham, that we might know more deeply the costliness of God's love for us.

Sacrificial Servant

*He made himself nothing by taking
the very nature of a servant, being
made in human likeness. And being
found in appearance as a man, he
humbled himself by becoming obedient
to death—even death on a cross!*

PHILIPPIANS 2:7–8 NIV

The life of Jesus from His humble birth to His death was a crescendo of sacrifice. The man who ultimately went to the cross was shaped by a lifetime of smaller sacrifices. True ministry is sacrifice. Perhaps it is so obvious that we miss it, but when Jesus gave His time to teach, to heal, to listen, to serve, it was time He wasn't spending on His comfort, His career, His memoirs, His mansion, or Himself. Daily sacrifice shapes us. It defines who we are and who we aren't. Jesus paid the ultimate sacrifice for us that we might be with Him in eternity. But upstream of that sacrifice was a life characterized by daily dying to self.

Motherhood is an opportunity to live into the rhythm of sacrifice. From rising early, to changing soiled diapers, to giving from our very bodies, to interrupted hours and interrupted nights, it is a training ground of sacrifice. Perhaps God is preparing us through these little moments of daily dying to self for a greater sacrifice. Or perhaps the servant posture will create the atmosphere in which your child grows and learns to be a leader by being the servant of all (Mark 9:35).

The man who became "obedient to death" began by being obedient to a sacrificial life. We would do well to do the same.

A Sacrifice of Joy

Let us run with endurance the race that is set before us, looking unto Jesus, the author and finisher of our faith, who for the joy that was set before Him endured the cross.
HEBREWS 12:1–2

All of us who endured the pain of labor know that once we hold that precious baby, the pain pales in comparison to the joy in our arms. While the pains of labor are nothing compared to the cross—and I don't mean to imply that—I think labor does give us an understanding of what the author of Hebrews meant when he said that Jesus endured the cross for the joy set before Him. Jesus could see the joy that bringing many sons and daughters into the kingdom would bring God the Father. Jesus could see the joy that salvation would bring to us. He could see what eternity in God's presence is like and all the good that awaits us.

Jesus set His eyes fixedly on this joy, like a runner sets his eyes on the finish line. And the writer of Hebrews told us to do the same. God does not idolize sacrifice like the stoics. Sacrifice was a means to an end, and the end itself is joy. Likewise, as God calls us into the life of sacrifice for the sake of others, it is not because He wants us to enjoy pain. He calls us to such sacrifices for the joy set before us. This is how we enter into the costly work of love. For the joy set before us we endure, we run, we persevere!

What was it like when you held your baby in your arms for the first time?

As mothers, our days are defined by a sacrificial posture toward our families. But when we work with our eyes set on teaching our young ones to love and honor God, how can that infuse our sacrifice with joy?

The Creativity of God

How many are your works, LORD!
In wisdom you made them all; the
earth is full of your creatures.
PSALM 104:24 NIV

*L*ike many I'm sure, I love a sunrise or sunset over the ocean. Once, I managed to see both in one day by driving from the east to the west coast in Florida. There are few things as stunning as the hues of coral, tangerine, peach, and lavender spreading out from or melting into the emerald-blue waters. Every day is a new sky canvas, and every shifting array of colors and clouds is as captivating as the last.

The earth is a continual display of God's endless creativity, testifying to His myriad attributes: the cobalt sky of His infinitude, the crystal dew of His mercies, the crashing waves of His faithfulness, the jutting mountains of His might, and the fathomless depths of His love. In Romans 1:20, Paul wrote, "For since the creation of the world God's invisible qualities—his eternal power and divine nature—have been clearly seen, being understood from what has been made, so that people are without excuse" (NIV). The created world testifies to a creative God and His manifold perfections. And I haven't even mentioned humanity. Have you stopped to marvel today at that little wonder God has given you? How does she reflect God's creativity? Think for a moment about your baby's absolute uniqueness. From the swirl of a tiny fingerprint to the sunrise of her smile, every facet of your darling reflects the infinite creativity of our God. Take a moment to marvel and worship today.

Creative Pursuers

To the weak I became as weak, that I might win the weak. I have become all things to all men, that I might by all means save some. Now this I do for the gospel's sake, that I may be partaker of it with you.

1 CORINTHIANS 9:22–23

Before your husband was your husband, perhaps he serenaded you beneath the dorm window or read your book club book just so he'd know what interested you. When you love someone, you pursue them. You think about who they are and what makes them tick. And then you find a way to pursue their heart in a way that is right for that heart.

When Jesus walked the earth, He wasn't pursuing hearts romantically, but He was pursuing hearts for His kingdom. And He paid attention to what the person before Him needed. To Zacchaeus, the tax collector, He pursued him by going to his house and having fellowship with the outcast. To the fisherman, Peter, He got his attention by flooding his boat with fish. Paul, later, did the same: to the weak, he became weak; to the Jew, as one under the law. As mothers, you have a lifetime ahead to pursue the heart of your child with the gospel with all the creativity and love God has given you. As Mama, you have an inside edge on that heart pursuit because you will know that child so deeply. It's never too early to start. Does your baby love music? Sing him songs about Jesus. Does he love to look at books? Get a simple board book about God's love. God's creative pursuit is our creative blueprint.

Our Creative Impulse

*For we are His workmanship, created
in Christ Jesus for good works,
which God prepared beforehand
that we should walk in them.*
EPHESIANS 2:10

With an eight-month-old, you may feel you have no time to be creative. I understand. But you can't help but be creative. You are made in the image of God. Our creativity is not simply reflected in the more artistic pursuits. We are being creative as we work, as we bring order to the chaos, in planning, in dreaming, and even in discipleship. Whatever season you are in, you can be creative.

You can take comfort in today's words from Ephesians 2:10. God has already prepared beforehand the good works He wants you to walk in. I'm not sure if you've ever experienced the fun of being in an art class where you walk in and the easel is ready, the canvas is set, the paints are out, the brushes are clean, and an apron is waiting for you on the stool. Well, God has prepped the studio for us in this way. He's gathered every material we need; He's provided the inspiration. All He asks is for our participation. Creativity takes faith out of our heads and into our hands. And it is a living act of hope—hope that transformation is possible. So whether your creativity today is bringing joy to your little one by blowing bubbles or plowing away at the presentation you have for the office or visiting a sick friend, know you are walking in God's good works prepared for you and bringing Him honor as you do it unto His glory!

In what ways has God made you a creative person? Tell your little one about it here.

Have you been on any fun or memorable outings with your baby? What places are you excited to take Baby one day?

Taste God's Goodness

Oh, taste and see that the LORD is good;
blessed is the man who trusts in Him!
PSALM 34:8

By this point, you are likely becoming an expert at the high-chair game of airplane. "Open wide! Zoom!" We may know how good a new food is, but sometimes we have to be creative when it comes to getting our babes to try it. It reminds me of the invitation in Psalm 34:8: "Oh, taste and see that the LORD is good." It is an invitation to come and experience God using the most sensory of language. It's almost as if the psalmist was saying, "Open your mouth; let's give this a try." It is an invitation to try God by trusting Him. God invites me to experience the goodness of God, which I can only truly know experientially by trying, trusting that God makes good things.

David continued this psalm by explaining that young lions go hungry, but "those who seek the LORD shall not lack any good thing" (34:10). In the verses that follow, David instructed us to try God's goodness by putting into practice His rules for living. It's almost as if he was saying, "Do you want to experience the goodness of God? Then trust Him, live by His ways, and you will taste and see that He is good." You will experience fullness better than the lions. You will not lack. You will know this as you live it. You will know this as you trust it. You will know this as you taste it. Knowing and trusting and tasting can't be separated.

The Intervening
Goodness of God

*Give thanks to the LORD, for he is good;
his love endures forever. Let the redeemed
of the LORD tell their story—those he
redeemed from the hand of the foe.*

PSALM 107:1–2 NIV

One way you show your love for your baby is by intervening in his life. Every time you keep him from picking up something that might cause him to choke, every time you come between your crawler and the stairs or reach out your hand to protect him from something hot, your goodness is intervening on his behalf. Proactively and reactively, you are constantly intervening.

Likewise, one of the big ways we see God's goodness is in His gracious interventions. Psalm 107 tells four stories of God's intervention. First, He intervenes on behalf of those searching for something to satisfy their emptiness: "For He satisfies the longing soul, and fills the hungry soul with goodness" (v. 9). Next, He intervenes for those who have despised the Word and experience suffering as a result. He leads "them out of darkness and the shadow of death, and [breaks] their chains in pieces" (v. 14). He also helps those whose mere foolishness leads them to sin. When they cry out He sends His word to heal and deliver. Finally, God helps those who suffer from calamity. God speaks peace into their storm. The psalmist beckoned all these to testify to the goodness of God, saying, "Oh, that men would give thanks to the LORD for His goodness" (v. 31). Oh, that we, too, would join in praise for His intervening goodness!

Be the Good

*Do not be overcome by evil, but
overcome evil with good.*
ROMANS 12:21

Perhaps you look around and feel overwhelmed: there's a stack of dishes in the sink, laundry and trash overflow, and you still haven't showered. The physical chaos merely echoes the emotional chaos of the weight of sickness, suffering, relational brokenness, injustice—in your life or those around you. But God is not ignorant of the evil around us. He is fully aware. And from the moment sin entered the world, God launched His counteroffensive, like the Allies' landing on the beaches of Normandy to overrun the Germans in WWII. We celebrate God's D-Day on Christmas. And He asks us to be part of the ongoing insurgence against evil. He doesn't give us a passive role to play but encourages our active raid on enemy territory. He charges us, "Do not be overcome by evil, but overcome evil with good."

Some may wonder about the problem of evil in the world. God answered the problem of evil with His Son's atoning death on the cross. This is what He has *done* about evil. And God wants to likewise answer the problem of evil in the world with His church. You and I, returning good for evil, we are the answer. You and I storming the sick wards with hope, we are God's answer. You and I, blitzing the depressed with encouragement, loosening the chains of the oppressed, raiding the lonesome with company, invading the darkness with light—we are God's answer to the problem of evil until that day when He finally obliterates sin, death, and suffering: until our ultimate victory.

How can you advance God's goodness today?

Sweet child of mine, I want to tell you of how God in His goodness has intervened in my life.

Craving a God of Justice

He is the Rock, His work is perfect;
for all His ways are justice, a God
of truth and without injustice;
righteous and upright is He.
DEUTERONOMY 32:4

Imagine a criminal whose crimes make the worst serial killer's pale in comparison. He is caught and brought before a judge. It takes weeks just to read a list of his crimes. And when the judge hears the case, he looks at the criminal and says, "I'm sure you didn't really mean it; I know you'll try harder next time. You are free to go." Can you imagine the outrage that would erupt? Can you imagine the protests and demands for that judge's job? You see, we are hardwired for justice. We want a world in which there is a penalty for wrong and reward for righteousness. It is ingrained in us because we are made in God's image. To have a God who is anything less than perfectly just would be a god who is not fit to reign.

In Deuteronomy, we have the first instance of God being called "the Rock." And it is certainly an immovable God we crave. We want to know there is a fixed point in the moral universe. We want Someone who will hold the wicked to account and who sees the acts of goodness done in secret. We do not want a god of whim and moral instability. As your child grows, he, too, will need you to be a mom of justice, a mom not governed by whim, but grounded in God's truth. You won't do this perfectly, but as you reflect the justice of God, even in how you respond to a dispute between your children, you will show that God cares about justice, even in the details of life.

The Obligation of Justice

Your Eight-Month-Old,
Week Four Theme:
Just

*For our sake he made him to be sin who
knew no sin, so that in him we might
become the righteousness of God.*

2 CORINTHIANS 5:21 ESV

a s His creations, the minimum we owed God from the beginning was complete obedience. When Adam and Eve bit into the forbidden fruit, justice cried out. Adam failed to meet God's standard, bringing the curse of death on all people.

For years, animal sacrifices like the sacrificial lamb pointed toward a perfect, but still unsatisfied, recompense to come. Before the last plague, God commanded Moses that the Israelites slaughter a spotless lamb and paint their doorways with the blood. Those who were "under" the blood of the lamb were saved. From that time on the Passover was the Israelites' biggest annual celebration. How beautifully symbolic, then, that Jesus, our ultimate Passover Lamb—born in a stable, worshiped by shepherds, wrapped in swaddling clothes (in which shepherds also wrapped spotless lambs set apart for sacrifice)—died during Passover week. Jesus, "who knew no sin," took our place, that justice and mercy might meet at the cross for us.

Don't miss this though. God's requirement of justice didn't just disappear; it was fulfilled in the sacrifice of Jesus. Likewise, as moms we can't simply ignore sin as our children grow. Justice cries out. But we can point our children to Jesus, who paid fully for every wrong we have done or will do on the cross. As we point them to Jesus' work on the cross, we teach them the tremendous consequences of sin *and* the grace God has shown us in His perfect Lamb.

Justice-Bearers

Learn to do right; seek justice. Defend the oppressed. Take up the cause of the fatherless; plead the case of the widow.
ISAIAH 1:17 NIV

If God is perfectly just, and if He has made us in His image, how do we bring His justice into this world?

God calls us to bring the light of truth where we see blatant injustice, and He wants us to model this for our kids. He does not want us to turn a blind eye. He wants us to stand up for the oppressed. He wants us to speak on behalf of the defenseless and the vulnerable. Not only can we speak up for them, but we can also be the love of Christ to those who experience the sting of injustice. As our children grow, they can take part in offering hospitality. They can help us make relief packages. We can even involve them as we make decisions about offering financial support.

Many people see injustice in the world and ask where God is. When the church is responding with the compassion and action that God intends for us to have, the world gets a front-row seat to God's response to evil and injustice—a response of love and compassion and care. But when the church abdicates its responsibility, the world assumes that God is indifferent to the plight of the oppressed. God has given you and your family a significant role in showing His heart to the world.

How is God's justice a comforting truth?

Does your baby have any special playmates, born around the same time, from nursery, playdates, or daycare?

Monthly Memories and Milestones

The biggest change for Baby lately has been . . .

_____

_____

_____

_____

What book do you enjoy reading to Baby? Why do you like reading it to your little one?

_____

_____

_____

_____

What song do you like to sing to Baby? What makes it special to you, and how does Baby respond?

_____

_____

_____

_____

Baby gets messiest when . . .

What sounds or words is Baby working on these days?

Other moments or milestones from this month:

Your Nine-Month-Old Developmental Guide

$\mathcal{A}$re you enjoying those gloriously chubby baby cheeks and thighs? At this stage, your baby may be having a growth spurt. Little boys on average weigh in at about 19.6 pounds, while little girls on average weigh about 18.1 pounds at nine months old. Those calories are also diversifying at this age with usually about half of your infant's calorie needs coming from table food and half coming from breastmilk or formula. If your little one is not taking to table foods as quickly as you'd hoped, don't be discouraged. It often takes introducing a food several times before your baby grows comfortable with it. Don't force your baby to finish a feeding; instead, allow her a chance to become familiar and comfortable with new foods through repeated exposure. Finger foods may be especially fun for her, as hand-eye coordination improves and independence grows. Feeding herself soft bits of veggies, small bites of pasta, cereals like Cheerios, or little bites of soft fruits may be just the challenge she wants.

You may also want to change the order of feedings, offering table foods before breast or formula feeds to allow your little one to have more of an appetite for trying new things. And while your baby does not need water outside of breastmilk or formula at this age, offering water in a sippy cup at mealtimes may help foods go down a bit easier. This is a great time for food experimentation: try to lean into the slowness of this baby stage and enjoy the delight and challenge of expanding tastes bit by bit.

Speaking of experimenting, your little one may be experimenting with new ways of mobility. Nine months is the average age for learning to crawl, so your baby may have been crawling for some time or may not be there yet. If your little one has been on the early curve, he may be pulling up on furniture, cruising, or taking first steps. If he is on the late end of the spectrum, sitting without support may be a more-recent development with core strength for crawling coming along right behind. Wherever he is, celebrate, support, and encourage.

Here are a few other milestones to be on the lookout for this month:

- Waves hello or bye-bye
- Says simple words like "Da" or "Ma"
- Babbles
- Stands unassisted
- Moves from stomach to seated position
- Creeps or crawls on the ground
- Walks or takes steps
- Moves toys from one hand to the other
- Grasps or pinches finger foods
- Enjoys opening and closing things
- "Plays" by rolling a ball back and forth or looking for hidden things
- Sees colors well
- Shows food preferences
- Demonstrates curiosity
- Shows separation anxiety

"Father": A Sensational Title.

My Father is working until now, and I am working.
JOHN 5:17 ESV

$\mathcal{H}$ as your baby started talking yet? "Da-da! Da-da!" I remember how thrilled I was when I heard my baby's first words so clearly. The tender name of "daddy" is a word we take for granted, especially when it comes to our heavenly Father. Through history there have been words that could get you arrested. But it's surprising that "My Father" are words that fall into that category. That simple, familiar address caused quite the uproar for Jesus. In fact, in the Gospels everything pivoted for Jesus' opponents after Jesus first publicly called God "My Father." What was so stunning about Jesus calling God "Father" is that it was totally unique.

A while ago a German New Testament scholar researched and ascertained that nowhere in writing does a Jewish person address God directly in the first person as Father—not anywhere in the history of Judaism, in all the Old Testament, in all extrabiblical Jewish writings—until the tenth century AD in Italy! Rabbis trained Jewish children how to properly address God: "Father" was never on the approved list. Jesus was the first Jewish rabbi to call God "Father" directly.[1] It was a radical departure from tradition, and in fact, in every recorded prayer we have from the lips of Jesus, save one, He called God "Father." Jesus was claiming an utterly unique relationship, and it caught His world aflame.

Our Father

*"In this manner, therefore, pray: Our
Father in heaven, hallowed be Your name."*

MATTHEW 6:9

$\mathcal{N}$ot only was it revolutionary for Jesus to address God as Father, but from the beginning He trained His followers to do the same. When you consider that this was not a way the Jews addressed God up to this point, it amplifies how special it is to call God by this name. In the Jewish context fatherhood implied a special relationship of care. There were duties implied and required of fathers: teaching the Torah, teaching a trade, circumcision, and even teaching a son to swim (since preservation of life was so fundamental). It was a given that a father would never forsake his child. To care, protect, and provide are fundamental roles of a father. But while Jesus has a right to call God "Father" by His nature as Son, we have this enormous privilege to call God "Father" by our redemption and subsequent adoption.

We've lost sight of the mind-blowing privilege to call God "Father." Mamas, you can enter His presence with that expectation of care, protection, and provision because of your status as adopted daughters. Today, you can come before God with the ease of a child and ask Him to help with the baby who is a fussy eater, or who is not developing properly, or who is teething and extra clingy. We can come with assurance that our Father will never abandon us. We are not orphans; we are under the care of a loving Father.

The Privilege of Adoption

For you did not receive the spirit of slavery to fall back into fear, but you have received the Spirit of adoption as sons, by whom we cry, "Abba! Father!"
ROMANS 8:15 ESV

As mothers one of our roles is to create a secure environment for our children. Feeling protected and safe in early childhood is key to their sense of safety and security for the rest of their lives. To do this, we create predictable routines and provide unconditional love.

Romans 8 opens and closes with reminders of our absolute security in Christ. "There is therefore now no condemnation to those who are in Christ Jesus," it begins. And it closes with the famous nothing-can-separate-us passage. Sandwiched in the middle is this profound truth of our adoption. While Jesus is God's Son by nature, we are His children through adoption. God did not make us servants, like the spoils of war. No. He adopted us. As His sons and daughters, we can cry out in a most intimate way, "Abba, Father," or "Daddy." This is not law or synagogue language; this is the language of home and hearth. We are invited into this intimacy and are secured an inheritance. We are heirs both now and in the world to come. God sings this lullaby over us—we are His.

How do you especially need to reach out to God and experience His care as Father to you today?

Dear one, I want to tell you about a good father I know . . .

A Careful Shepherd

The LORD is my shepherd; I shall not want.
PSALM 23:1

While the concept of God as our shepherd is a foundational metaphor for knowing God, it is also overly familiar. We need to look with fresh eyes to see the riches God has for us in this term.

A shepherd in Palestine was responsible for leading the sheep to find good pasture. Rich grass wasn't a given; poor pasture produced malnourished, sickly sheep. The shepherd also had to find a water source that was not so rapid as to carry the sheep away, nor so still as to be stagnant. Leading them involved making sure none strayed, including the weak, the nursing ewes, and their young. Wild beasts—lions, bears, and panthers—were a real danger. Bands of thieves also preyed on those in desolate places. At night, the shepherd did not get to clock out at 5:00 p.m. The sheep needed protection through the night.

In a real sense, the character, skill, and expertise of the shepherd determined the welfare of an individual sheep. To have an unskilled or careless shepherd meant almost certain harm. When David said "the Lord is my shepherd," it was equivalent to saying that the most careful, conscientious, strong, resourceful, and skilled caregiver is my overseer. Because God is my shepherd, I shall not experience any lack in my care. As moms, we can learn a lot from the model of God as our Good Shepherd. Careful, conscientious, strong, resourceful, and skilled should be qualities we emulate in caring for the precious lambs God has entrusted to our care.

A Good Shepherd

Ah, shepherds of Israel who have
been feeding yourselves! Should
not shepherds feed the sheep?

EZEKIEL 34:2 ESV

The bad has a way of making us appreciate the good. And the people of Israel certainly experienced some bad shepherds!

Through the prophet Ezekiel, God pronounced woe on Israel's leaders, who had shirked their responsibilities to protect and guide His people. In contrast to their lack of care, God promised within Ezekiel 34 to seek out, feed, gather, strengthen, provide, and protect. Furthermore, He promised to make a covenant of peace, banish wild beasts, send down showers, break His people's yoke, deliver them, and make them dwell securely. Through this "they shall know that I the LORD am their God with them" (Ezekiel 34:30 ESV). These are huge and beautiful promises. Like a good shepherd, God's presence with His people is integral to their well-being. It is a job that requires personal, present attention.

When Jesus later called Himself the "Good Shepherd," the Jews would have heard it as a messianic fulfillment of the prophecies in this chapter (John 10:11, 14). In Jesus, literally our God-with-us Emmanuel, God shepherds His people with personal, up-close care. Like our Good Shepherd, we are to give personal, present attention to our little lambs. As Christ became our God-with-us, we, too, are called to enter the world of our little ones: they should know a mom-with-us care—whether that's getting down on the floor and playing blocks or offering cuddles in the midst of teething pain. As they grow, keeping this *with-them* attention will go a long way to helping them understand the heart of their Good Shepherd.

A Seeking Shepherd

What do you think? If a man has a hundred sheep, and one of them has gone astray, does he not leave the ninety-nine on the mountains and go in search of the one that went astray?

MATTHEW 18:12 ESV

When I was about three, I gave my parents quite the scare. We were at home when my parents realized it had been a while since they'd seen me. We lived on a river, so after a few minutes of searching, they began to panic. Thankfully, someone happened to glance between the family room couch and the wall and saw that I had crawled into that tight little spot and fallen asleep!

Knowing my parents' love for me, I can't imagine them deciding to just give up. Likewise, in this passage we see that the Good Shepherd's heart for the lost is one of relentless love. He does everything in His power to seek and save the lost. Though the terrain is wide, though the sheep is elusive, though dangers are grave, He will not give up. No distance is too great, no life too far gone, no case too complicated. Like our Good Shepherd we need to have a heart for the lost sheep in our lives. And we should also think of the seeking shepherd as we parent. Even now, we can begin by relentlessly praying for our children to know God and giving them the gifts of our eyes, our attention, and our delight. As the years unfold, you can look to Deuteronomy 6:7 as a guide for how to keep on seeking their hearts, teaching them diligently throughout the day. Persistently seeking, passionately loving—that's our God for us and our model.

A shepherd's job, like a mother's, requires constant attention and vigilance. As you shepherd your baby, how is it comforting to know that God is shepherding you?

Dear little lamb, your mama has seen you do some silly things. Like a sheep, you sometimes get into trouble and have a hard time getting out of it! Let me tell you about how . . .

Everlasting

Before the mountains were born
or You gave birth to the earth and
the world, even from everlasting
to everlasting, You are God.
PSALM 90:2 NASB

Your life before Baby and after Baby will never be quite the same, especially if this is your first child. Perhaps you traveled for work more, had more room for spontaneity, or spent more time on your hobbies. As our kids grow, it's hard for them to imagine Mom and Dad had a life and a love story before they were born. In this psalm attributed to Moses, he contemplated the life of God before the "birth" of the mountains and the earth. He realized that God is everlasting, without beginning or end, and that His character is unchanging.

Like the psalmist, it is good for us to contemplate that we are part of a love that precedes us and that is eternal. Our triune God is an everlasting God. And the love that existed within the Trinity began long before time. There is something incredibly comforting in that. Before the mountains and earth, God was. And when we return to dust, God will be. And in the interim, we can enjoy God deeply. With the psalmist, we can pray, "Satisfy us in the morning with your unfailing love, that we may sing for joy and be glad all our days" (Psalm 90:14 NIV). God's everlasting nature—His love that precedes and follows us—surrounds us and gives us reason to take joy in the moment and be glad.

Everlasting Benefits

*Do you not know? Have you not
heard? The Everlasting God, the
LORD, the Creator of the ends of the
earth does not become weary or tired.
His understanding is inscrutable.*

ISAIAH 40:28 NASB 1995

$\mathcal{A}$s mamas, we know bone tired. We know weary. We know what it is to be bound by our finite bodies in time. God, on the other hand, is not bound by time. He is not finite. He is eternal and everlasting. Does this impact our lives? Absolutely.

The prophet Isaiah offered us words of comfort in today's verse based on God's everlasting nature. Because God is everlasting and exists outside of time, He does not grow weary or tired. In a world of babies who keep us up at all hours and require from us more than we feel we can give, it is reassuring to know that our God will not say, "Sorry, can you try to pray to Me tomorrow when I've been able to catch up on some sleep?" Our God isn't only half-listening because He is so worn out.

Because God exists outside of time, all moments are present to Him. We see time like a parade. He sees it like He's above the parade viewing it all at once. And because of this, His understanding is truly beyond what we can fathom. He sees the beginning, the middle, and the end of our stories all at once, because He is not hedged in by a beginning or an end. His understanding is truly inscrutable.

What Is Eternal?

These will go away into
eternal punishment, but the
righteous into eternal life.
MATTHEW 25:46 NASB

This week we've reflected on God's everlasting nature. "From everlasting to everlasting" is our God, wrote Moses in Psalm 90:2. We've thought about how God has no beginning and is not bound by time. But today as we think about what it means for God to be "from everlasting to everlasting," let's focus on the other end of this equation: eternity to come.

Because God will last forever and created some things that will likewise last forever, certain things have an eternal value. Some things will pass away and some will remain. We need to be constantly examining our priorities, plans, and goals. Some things will not last. Promotions, farmhouse sinks, and big backyards will not make the cut of eternity. Human souls will. Someday those who know Him will live with Him forever, while those who do not will face eternal punishment. In light of this, we must examine our lives closely. Are we sharing the gospel and giving ourselves to things of eternal significance? If not, why? As you mother, remember that you are doing something with an eternal value. You are shepherding a human soul. In the monotony and minutiae of motherhood, don't lose sight of your high and holy calling to model the love of Jesus, to teach God's truths to your children from their infancy, and to model sacrificial love. As you build your home around these truths, you are investing into eternity.

Everlasting—what comfort do you take from God's everlasting nature?

Sweet baby, let me tell you how Mommy and Daddy's love story began . . .

The Beauty of God

*One thing have I asked of the L*ORD*,*
that will I seek after: that I may dwell
*in the house of the L*ORD *all the days of*
my life, to gaze upon the beauty of the
*L*ORD *and to inquire in his temple.*
PSALM 27:4 ESV

Beauty is difficult to define. We know what it does to us. It's the way the swelling crescendo of a symphony moves us. It's the way the colors of a painting awe us. It's the way a canyon aglow takes our breath away. Beauty calls to us from symmetry, color, harmony, mastery, skill, grace, excellence, and goodness. We ache for beauty and ache to be truly beautiful. Advertisers know it. They manipulate us with clever ads that whisper, "If you buy this, you will be beautiful." These ploys work because our longing for beauty is so strong. Why?

We long for beauty because we long for God. God is the source of everything good and beautiful. And one day that longing for beauty will be fully sated as we gaze upon God. In the meantime, as moms in post-baby bodies, it's easy to chase illusive cultural ideals of beauty. But while it's good to be healthy, and beauty has its place, we don't have to get on the treadmill of the world's overblown value of personal beauty. Our hearts can rest knowing that the lifelong craving for beauty will be satisfied as we turn our gaze fully upon Him: infinite in His perfections, beautiful in His holiness, radiant in His glory. We will behold the beauty our souls crave and be made like Him.

The Beauty of God's Perfection

Out of Zion, the perfection of
beauty, God will shine forth.
PSALM 50:2

$\mathcal{M}$ost mothers I know think their babies are perfect. I am no exception. Each of my babies has been perfectly beautiful to me. But while we mothers may not be able to be objective when it comes to our offspring, there exists a reality of perfection that all lesser beauties point us toward. Our hearts leap at perfection. Whether it is the perfectly executed triple lutz of the Olympic figure skater, the way a surfer conquers a wave, or that breathtaking moment as the curtain falls on a stunning performance, there is something of beauty in perfection.

God is the perfection of all moral attributes; He is perfectly good, perfectly righteous, perfectly holy, perfectly just, perfectly merciful, and more. When we say that God is beautiful, it is another way to say that He is perfect in every way. His acts and being are perfection—no one comes close. Imagine the breathtaking beauty of One whose being is perfect in every way. Like a diamond of infinite facets, the radiance of His perfect beauty shines forth. No wonder the book of Revelation tells us, "The city does not need the sun or the moon to shine on it, for the glory of God gives it light, and the Lamb is its lamp" (21:23 NIV). The radiance of God's beautiful, multifaceted perfection shines forth for all eternity.

The Beauty of the Bride

*So that he might present the church
to himself in splendor, without spot
or wrinkle or any such thing, that she
might be holy and without blemish.*
EPHESIANS 5:27 ESV

As we've thought about the beauty of God, we've considered how our hearts are made with a longing for beauty. Not only do we ache for beauty, but we also ache to be beautiful. After pregnancy, we often pursue the ache with abandon, seeking to transform ourselves with the latest diet and exercise regimen and an updated wardrobe if we can afford it. But while outward beauty is not without value, it pales in comparison to the beauty of a soul satisfied in God. As Peter reminded us, "Do not let your adorning be external . . . but let your adorning be the hidden person of the heart with the imperishable beauty of a gentle and quiet spirit" (1 Peter 3:3–4 ESV).

At the end of time, the church will be presented to Jesus as a radiant bride. Do you remember how much time you spent getting ready for your wedding? Maybe someone helped to fix your hair. Perhaps you exercised or dieted for months to fit into your dress. As the bride of Christ, we ready ourselves in anticipation of that ultimate wedding day. But God longs for us to make our hearts beautiful with the beauty of a gentle and quiet spirit. A gentle spirit is patient, kind, and forgiving. A quiet spirit is one that rests in the Lord to care for us. We long to be beautiful; let us prioritize lasting beauty as we ready ourselves for the great wedding day by cultivating a gentle and quiet spirit.

Mothering doesn't leave us much time to take care of ourselves. How does knowing that God values you deeply make you feel secure in a world that puts so much emphasis on physical beauty?

What new skills is your baby mastering these days?

Monthly Memories and Milestones

Baby is moving these days by . . .

_____

_____

_____

Baby likes to say . . .

_____

_____

_____

Baby tried to . . .

_____

_____

_____

Baby's first home was . . .

_____

_____

_____

In looking at old baby pictures, I think Baby looks most like . . .

Baby's favorite foods these days include . . .

My favorite thing I've gotten to do with Baby recently was . . .

Your Ten-Month-Old Developmental Guide

While the world opens for your ten-month-old, you may find it's also a time of growing frustration for him. Your little one is eager to go places but may not quite have the coordination or may be afraid of being far from you. He is eager to communicate but may not yet have the words. He is forming opinions on foods and toys but may struggle to share what makes him happy or sad. And he may want to push the boundaries but is receiving a firm "no" from you or Dad when curiosity is pushing him into danger or negative behavior.

Because of these factors, you may be experiencing a growth curve with your parenting skills. You may be learning to say a firm "no" for the first time to a suddenly willful little one. You are learning how to help coach her without doing it for her. For instance, when you see your child struggling to do something, resist the urge to immediately swoop in and do it for her. Give her time to struggle and try the new task before coming to her aid. This is a balancing act; wait too long, and she is frustrated and in tears. Swoop in too early, and she is not developing her growing skills. You'll be walking that line for a lifetime, so it's good to start getting experience now.

Use play to connect and help your child grow in the skills he needs. For example, pointing to pictures or objects and saying their names, while giving him a chance to make a sound back, is a great way to encourage vocal experimentation and learning. Putting an interesting toy under a blanket or holding it just out of reach can be a fun way to encourage exploration and mobility. Wherever your little one is, you can be the coach and cheerleader to get him to the next step. Speaking of milestones, here are a few to watch for this month:

- Sits for long periods without toppling
- Is crawling
- Picks up objects using pincer grasp
- Says "Mama" or "Dada"
- Stacks toys like blocks or cups
- Squats from a standing position or pulls up from a sitting position
- Rolls front to back and back to front
- Understands simple commands or phrases
- Shows separation anxiety
- Shows curiosity
- Shows preferences for tastes or toys

Redeemer

*But we had hoped that he was
the one to redeem Israel.*

LUKE 24:21 ESV

Cleopas and another disciple were walking to Emmaus shortly after the death of Christ. Imagine their grief; the man whom they thought would redeem their people had died that week, arrested and executed like a scandalous criminal. There had been resurrection rumors, but could they believe it? As they walked, a man joined them, and as he explained the Scriptures, their hearts burned within them. Finally, over broken bread, their eyes were opened: this was their Jesus—the one they had hoped would "redeem" Israel.

Ironically, He *had* redeemed Israel, but what did that mean? According to Mosaic law, a redeemer had the duty of restoring the rights of another and avenging his wrongs. For instance, if an indebted Israelite needed to sell his land, it could be redeemed by a close relative for a price. That person became the redeemer of the land; he paid a debt he did not owe to restore someone else's loss. This is what Christ did on the cross. We owed a debt for breaking God's commandments. We had lost unhampered relationship with God, eternal life, and holiness. Christ Himself paid the debt and restored our loss. He redeemed us!

Mamas, amid the responsibilities of motherhood, maybe it's been a while since your heart burned within you. But remember Christ met these disciples in the midst of their dejection, at their ordinary tasks. If you need your heart to burn again in wonder, ask Him to meet you on your road. He can.

Redeemed for a Purpose

*For if while we were enemies we were
reconciled to God by the death of his
Son, much more, now that we are
reconciled, shall we be saved by his life.*
ROMANS 5:10 ESV

Imagine, out of love, you took the place of a man on death row. Then imagine that man was released and returned to a life of crime. You didn't redeem his life back for him to squander it. Likewise, Christ has bought us back for a purpose. His life was given for your life to be fully lived.

God has redeemed *you* for a purpose, and one of the purposes for which He has redeemed you is to be a mother. Yes, many moms mother on autopilot. But mothering with intentionality and an eye toward shepherding your child to love Christ is no small calling. God has entrusted you with the care of a human soul. And while He may call you to more, He certainly hasn't called you to less. Yes, today, your child may be too young to hear and understand the deep truths of the faith. But she is not too young to internalize your love and care, something that has a profound impact. It's also not too early for you to prepare your heart to share these deep truths. Lord willing, you have many years ahead to share God's character. But by as early as nine, most children's habits are set.[1] That means these early years are a crucial window to shape the habits of the heart: habits of reading the Word together, praying, practicing obedience, and serving gladly. Where do you need to strengthen your own faith and understanding for the task before you?

A Future Redemption

Not only that, but we also who have the firstfruits of the Spirit, even we ourselves groan within ourselves, eagerly waiting for the adoption, the redemption of our body.
ROMANS 8:23

My mom suffered from polio as a little girl. She was paralyzed in her right leg at three years old, and the doctors thought she would never walk again. By God's grace, she did, but she still suffers the residual effects. Perhaps you or a loved one suffers a physical reminder that our redemption isn't complete. We have tasted the firstfruits of redemption by the Spirit; we know hope through Christ, but there is a fullness of redemption still to come. Theologians call this the "already and not yet" nature of the gospel.

Paul did not minimize these sufferings. In fact, he knew such intimately: beaten with rods, stoned and left for dead, imprisoned, and whipped. We can be sure that he bore the scars. But Paul stated boldly, "I consider that the sufferings of this present time are not worthy to be compared with the glory which shall be revealed in us" (Romans 8:18). Where are you groaning today for redemption? We all struggle in different ways, whether it's extremes of postpartum depression or anxiety, or the mundane disappointments of mothering in a fallen world. But this future redemption gives us hope, even on our hardest days. Like Paul, we can believe these present sufferings will dim in comparison to future glory. And we know that if God did not spare His own Son (8:31–32), He will do everything it takes to bring about this final redemption.

Do you think our culture places much value on the calling of motherhood? How do you see yourself mothering with intentionality in the years to come?

What are you enjoying about Baby these days?

A Refining God

*For you, God, tested us; you
refined us like silver.*
PSALM 66:10 NIV

$\mathcal{A}$ s mamas, it's difficult to watch our babies go through pain, whether it's the mild discomfort of teething, the falls of early attempts to pull up, or the ordinary illnesses we'll see them go through. When they experience such trials, big or small, our hearts are with them.

In biblical times, silver was purified in fire to melt away the dross. A silversmith would never leave the fire unattended, for the silver could burn up easily, but he would hold the silver in the hottest part of the fire and know it was done when he could see his reflection in the metal. As you walk through trials as a mom, know that God's heart is with you, just like your heart is with your little one. God is careful with us. Through our trials, He never leaves us. As the prophet Malachi stated, "He will sit as a smelter and purifier of silver" (Malachi 3:3 NASB). In other words, He stays with us. He permits the intensity of the trials, but with purpose and never longer than necessary. He does not test us haphazardly. He tests us to purify us, to refine us, to make His image shine forth in us. It is a mark of His love that He does not leave us as we are but disciplines those whom He loves (Hebrews 12:6–7). He refines and sanctifies us until His image shines forth clearly in us.

Refined for His Glory

Behold, I have refined you, but not as
silver; I have tested you in the furnace
of affliction. For My own sake, for
My own sake, I will act. . . . And I
will not give My glory to another.

ISAIAH 48:10–11 NASB

*B*abies can be demanding. They can't put the needs of others before their own. Developmentally, they live in a baby-centric universe. As your child grows, he will learn the world doesn't revolve around him.

There is One, however, who is rightfully the center of our universe. Since God is completely worthy of all glory, it is right for Him to be totally committed to seeking it. So when God says that for His own name's sake He will refine us and test us, it is not arrogance. It is fitting. We are made for His glory. We are made to reflect His image. And when we fail to do so, particularly when we claim to be His but sin grievously, we profane His name.

But while God is committed to refining the Israelites for His glory, His glory is also their greatest good. To be conformed into His image is the path of abundant life. God longs for that abundance for us: "Oh that you had paid attention to my commandments! Then your peace would have been like a river" (48:18 ESV). He longs for the trials to bring His people back to His ways that they might know blessing. For Him to be committed to His own glory is for Him to be committed to our greatest good.

Joy in Our Refinement

[Know] that the testing of your faith produces patience. But let patience have its perfect work, that you may be perfect and complete, lacking nothing.
JAMES 1:3–4

When my niece was little, her siblings nicknamed her *Wreck-o-saurus*. Likewise, your baby may be pulling books off the shelves, admiring gravity as green peas drop from the high chair, and otherwise leaving mayhem in her wake. In the meantime, you are earning a degree in patience as your Wreck-o-saurus helps refine you. This week we've examined how God refines and purifies us. He does it because He loves us, as a father disciplines his son because he loves him (Hebrews 12:6). He refines us for His own name's sake, for His own glory (Isaiah 48:9–11). And today we see that He refines us for our own completeness, that we might be perfect, whole, and lacking nothing.

God has laid out for you a refining course. The obstacles in the years ahead might look somewhat ordinary: meltdowns and tantrums, night terrors, bed-wetting, and everyday sibling rivalry battles. It may surprise you to realize that amid the everyday messy and mundane highs and lows of motherhood, He is, like a trainer, guiding your route to make you holy and whole. Athletes navigate obstacle courses to train for earthly medals. How much more should we count it a joy knowing God is refining our very souls—not for a medal but to present us at the revelation of Jesus Christ as a glorious, beautiful bride! Let us trust the refiner and count it all joy that we've been chosen to be made complete for His glory!

How have you seen God use the challenges of early motherhood to refine you?

Is your baby enjoying any board books or special toys these days?

Our Passionate God

How can I give you up, Ephraim? How can I hand you over, Israel? How can I make you like Admah? How can I set you like Zeboiim? My heart churns within Me; My sympathy is stirred.

HOSEA 11:8

Every passing day, your bonds with Baby grow. From first smiles to first foods, from first laughs to first army crawls, as you cheer your baby on through the milestones, your hearts are bound together. One of my favorite Bible passages is the eleventh chapter of Hosea. In this chapter, we see that God has loved His people from the beginning; like a loving parent, He has taught us to walk, led us with "gentle cords," and even bent down to feed us (11:1, 3–4). But despite all His love, we are "bent on backsliding" (11:7). But God doesn't give up on us. He wonders aloud how He can give us up or treat us as we deserve. His heart recoils at the thought and His compassion is aroused (11:8). He chooses not to come to us in the wrath we deserve, but instead to pursue us: "He will roar like a lion; when he roars, his children shall come trembling from the west" (11:10 ESV).

The passion of God for us in this chapter is truly awe-inspiring. He doesn't give up. He doesn't let go. He doesn't stop calling. He desires to be with us. As you hold your baby today and reflect on your passionate love for this infant, let it lead you to behold the wonder of the infinitely greater passion of God for you both. Let that love bind you to Him for all your days.

His Passionate Son

Your Ten-Month-Old,
Week Three Theme:
Passionate

*O Jerusalem, Jerusalem, the one who
kills the prophets and stones those who
are sent to her! How often I wanted
to gather your children together, as
a hen gathers her chicks under her
wings, but you were not willing!*

MATTHEW 23:37

Just as the longing heart of God can be heard through the words of Hosea 11 in yesterday's passage, today we hear Christ's longing heart as He looks out over the city of Jerusalem. Jesus looks on it with so much love and compares His longing to a mother hen's heart to gather her chicks beneath her wings. These are God's chosen people: descended from the ones who were led on the Red Sea road, who were sustained with manna in the wilderness, who tried His patience at Sinai, who seized the promised land, who forgot His ways in the time of the judges, who clamored for a king, and who later were scattered in exile in hopes that they would return to Him. And now, as Christ prepared for His final weeks on this earth, He lamented over His children. How He longed to gather them into His arms; how He longed for them to come home to Him.

This motherly metaphor bespeaks volumes of Christ's passionate heart for His people, Israel, and for all His children who have turned their backs on Him. He longs for them. He longs for us. How Christ echoes the heart of His Father in His love for us! Mamas, if you ever doubt God's goodness, go with Jesus up to this hill over Jerusalem and hear the parental affection as He weeps for you. He loves you. He longs to bring you close.

Passionate Parenting

And he arose and came to his father.
But while he was still a long way off, his
father saw him and felt compassion, and
ran and embraced him and kissed him.

LUKE 15:20 ESV

As we've seen this week, it's notable that when God wants to describe His passionate heart for us, He often chooses parenthood as the guiding metaphor. In Hosea 11, we read about God teaching Israel to walk, feeding and leading her, and then lamenting over her waywardness. In Matthew 23, Jesus longs for us like a mother hen. And when He wants to teach us to have a heart for others, He shows us the parental affection of the prodigal's father.

Have you ever looked at this story from the father's point of view? While the younger son squandered his inheritance in reckless living, the father waited with longing. He must have been scanning the horizon daily, watching for his son, because while the young man was still a long way, he ran and embraced him. He lavished His love on him.

If God has so much to say about His passionate heart for us through the metaphor of parenthood, it behooves us to pay attention to the moments He might want to whisper to our hearts in everyday life. Your love for your child, albeit imperfect, can be a window to wonder at the heart of God. As your child grows, his disobedience can serve as a mirror for how we, too, turn away from the Father's love. And as you long to give your child good gifts, it's but a picture of God's generosity toward us. Let His passionate heart for His children shape your own!

Passion comes from the root "to suffer" or "to endure." As mothers, our passionate love for our children will lead us to suffer alongside them, to hurt when they hurt, to care deeply for them in all their troubles and heartaches. We can endure with them because Christ endures with us. How does Christ's willingness to suffer alongside you strengthen you to come alongside your child?

How has your baby already taught you something about God or life?

Truth

"I am the LORD, and there is no other.
I did not speak in secret, in a land of
darkness; I did not say to the offspring
of Jacob, 'Seek me in vain.' I the LORD
speak the truth; I declare what is right."
ISAIAH 45:18–19 ESV

$\mathcal{A}$ s a mother, your view of truth has a huge impact on how you parent and raise your child. We live in an age, however, where a statement as patently obvious as "there is truth, and it is knowable" is rejected. But humanity has a long history of suppressing the plain truth. In fact, Paul noted that since the beginning, people have suppressed "the truth by their wickedness, since what may be known about God is plain to them, because God has made it plain to them" (Romans 1:18–19 NIV).

But God is emphatic about truth. He hasn't hidden it. He's made it clear: "For since the creation of the world God's invisible qualities . . . have been clearly seen, being understood from what has been made, so that men are without excuse" (v. 20 NIV). In Isaiah, God tells us that He did not speak in secret. He hasn't sought to hide things, but instead He has revealed Himself and made the world knowable. If there was not ultimate truth, it would be vain to seek God. But the truth is knowable, and in His mercy He promised, "You will seek me and find me when you seek me with all your heart" (Jeremiah 29:13 NIV).

Will you pray for someone the Lord brings to mind who is actively suppressing the plain truths of who He is? Pray that God would open her eyes to the ways His invisible qualities are clearly seen around her.

The Way, the Truth, and the Life

Jesus said to him, "I am the way, and the truth, and the life. No one comes to the Father except through me."

JOHN 14:6 ESV

*D*oes your little one hate being separated from you? Separation anxiety is so hard. Helping him work through his fears may be the first of many times you help your child manage emotions. In John 14, Thomas was having a bit of separation anxiety as Christ talked about His departure. Thomas naturally wondered how he could follow if he didn't know where Jesus was going. Thomas needed the facts. Jesus explained that He is the way to the Father; no one can come to the Father except through Him. Jesus is "the way, and the truth, and the life."

Notice Jesus doesn't say He is *a* way. He says He is *the* way. He doesn't say He is *a* truth. He says He is *the* truth. And He doesn't say He is *one* way of living. He says He is *the* life. Today some may call this passage narrow-minded. But look how wide Jesus opens this door—through His death and resurrection, *anyone* who believes may not only know the way to God but follow the way to a reconciled relationship with God. He has made truth knowable, findable, and attainable. And He offers not just any life but abundant life freely to all who believe. In our separation anxiety, Jesus does not leave us alone. He shows us the way home.

Knowing Truth Through His Word

To the Jews who had believed him, Jesus said, "If you hold to my teaching, you are really my disciples. Then you will know the truth, and the truth will set you free."
JOHN 8:31–32 NIV

Regarding truth, God has not set us up for failure. He has given us everything we need to know, to understand, to walk in, and teach truth to our children. He has given us His Word (Psalm 119:160); Jesus, the Word made flesh (John 1:14); and "the Spirit of truth" to "guide [us] into all truth" (John 16:13). As moms, this is a great comfort: we aren't on our own in knowing truth, applying it, or teaching it to our children; we have the Word and Spirit to guide us. And as we come to know the truth, it sets us free.

In the years ahead, as you read and discuss God's Word with your child, remember you aren't teaching them a rule book. You are opening an invitation to grace. They can't keep these commands perfectly; that's why they need a Savior who will set them free. God invites us in the most abundant, joyful, life-giving way possible. God makes the way clear, but that doesn't mean we can expect to grow automatically. We are to earnestly seek Him (Psalm 145:18), ask Him to guide us in truth (Psalm 25:5), ask Him to teach us truth (Psalm 86:11), and learn to handle the Word of truth correctly (2 Timothy 2:15). Ask God today to help you pursue His truth, that you might know and share His freedom!

Because we are believers, the Holy Spirit guides us in all truth. How is it comforting to know that you aren't alone as you seek to teach truth to your children?

What skills has your baby been developing lately?

Monthly Memories and Milestones

My favorite thing Baby has outgrown is . . .

_____

_____

_____

Baby's favorite part of this season of the year so far has been . . .

_____

_____

_____

_____

So far Baby has ___ teeth. His favorite things to chomp on with them have been . . .

_____

_____

_____

_____

Baby's typical day consists of . . .

Other moments or milestones from this month . . .

Your Eleven-Month-Old Developmental Guide

*J*ust eleven months ago, a nurse was giving you your newborn's measurements. By now your baby may have nearly tripled his birth weight (average: 19.2 pounds for a girl, 20.8 pounds for a boy), and instead of measuring his length stretched prone, today you can see how tall he is! Pulling up or standing upright is a more common position these days than those early days stretched out on a blanket or floor mat! Break out that wall growth chart; those toddler days are just around the corner.

As you near that first birthday milestone, your emotions may be all over the map. Some moms are relieved to see days of more independence on the horizon. Other moms mourn the loss of the infant days. But most moms experience some range of emotions, from excitement at the independence to come to sadness over the days you'll leave behind. Give yourself permission to feel what you feel, and take those highs and lows to God.

Speaking of highs and lows, you may find your little one is able to reach into more unexpected places as little by little his range of motion goes from what is at crawling level to what is at standing (or even climbing) level. Keep babyproofing ahead of those milestones. Milestones this month could include the following:

- Crawling
- Standing unassisted
- Taking assisted or independent steps or cruising around furniture
- Pointing or moving toward desired items or toys
- Grabbing finger foods
- Stacking play items
- Experiencing separation anxiety
- Saying words like *Mama* or *Dada*
- Imitating animal sounds
- Enjoying music and dancing
- Understanding simple commands or phrases

As you look ahead with excitement to that first birthday, try not to hold yourself to standards of birthday party perfection. Some babies may enjoy parties and crowds; others may not. Just remember: your celebration doesn't need to be big or fancy; it doesn't need to be perfect. But do plan to take time to celebrate God's goodness in your life through the blessing of this very special child and all the wonder he has brought into your world.

Jehovah Rapha, My Healer

I am the LORD who heals you.
EXODUS 15:26

For some reading this, Christian mothering may be pioneering work; you may not have had models of Jesus growing up. For others, maybe your parents showed you the way, but others have let you down, deeply wounding you. All of us have broken places and deep needs for healing. Our God, however, desires for us to have wholeness of mind, body, and spirit.

In the wilderness, God first made Himself known to the Israelites as Jehovah Rapha. This very personal, intimate name for God means "the Lord who heals you." He showed the Israelites His heart to do them good as they stood before the bitter waters of Marah, and He turned them sweet. This was a foreshadowing of the living waters, offered in Christ (John 7:37) and flowing in eternity (Revelation 22:17).

God doesn't want to leave us where we are. He desires to bring us wholeness. We hear His heart for His wayward people in Isaiah, when He said, "I have seen his ways, and will heal him; I will also lead him, and restore comforts to him. . . . 'And I will heal him'" (57:18–19). What wounds does God want you to bring to Him today in prayer? Which places need healing so you can be the best parent possible? What a comfort to know that God wants to bring healing to our deepest hurts!

Christ's Healing Mission

Your Eleven-Month-Old,
Week One Theme:
Healer

*He has sent me to proclaim liberty
to the captives and recovering of
sight to the blind, to set at liberty
those who are oppressed, to proclaim
the year of the Lord's favor.*

LUKE 4:18–19 ESV

When Jesus began His earthly ministry after John had baptized Him in the Jordan, He went to Nazareth, and on the Sabbath in the synagogue He opened the scroll of Isaiah and read the words above. He then sat down and said, "Today this Scripture has been fulfilled in your hearing" (Luke 4:21 ESV). Jesus' earthly ministry was full of these foretastes of the kingdom to come: opening the eyes of the blind, healing the brokenhearted, setting the captives free. Everywhere He went, He preached, He healed, and He brought freedom. In this we see authentication of His role as Messiah and God's own Son. And in it we also get a foretaste of the world to come.

Likewise, we are to be ministers of His healing. One of the translations of the word *heal* is "to serve" (Matthew 12:15). We are to be Christ's serving hands in our communities. Even with a baby in tow, you can play a role in healing the brokenhearted. You can visit a local nursing home perhaps; babies bring such cheer! Or you can serve the sick by dropping off a meal for a family facing illness. As our children grow, we can teach them to pray for the sick in our community. God shapes their hearts through compassionate prayers for others. God has called us to be a part of His ongoing healing and serving ministry until He comes again. Ask Him how He would have you continue His mission today.

Our Ultimate Healing

Through the middle of the street of the city;
also, on either side of the river, [was] the
tree of life with its twelve kinds of fruit,
yielding its fruit each month. The leaves of
the tree were for the healing of the nations.
REVELATION 22:2 ESV

a dear friend has struggled with chronic illness for over two decades, robbing her of the ability to work, to invest in relationships, often to attend church or serve, and even to enjoy simple pleasures like hiking. I was texting her recently that I cannot wait to run with her in the world to come. I picture us running, laughing, and enjoying healed bodies. Obviously, I don't exactly know what eternity will be like, but I do know that God will give us new bodies (1 Corinthians 15:42) and heal us in body, mind, and spirit.

Revelation 22:2 talks about a street running along a river, with a tree of life blooming with twelve kinds of fruit and leaves for healing the nations. In Revelation 21:4, we have the promise "death shall be no more, neither shall there be mourning, nor crying, nor pain anymore" (ESV). A promised wholeness is coming. It has begun now through our salvation, but it will be completed in eternity. We will receive incorruptible bodies. Babies, with their fresh skin, not wrinkled or marred by time, whisper to us of a hope when we, too, will have a brand-new body and all things will be made new. We will be fresh, without wounds of heart and soul. We will be healed. These are the promises of hope that get us through the hard days. Our God is Jehovah Rapha, the one who heals!

God is our healer. How is this name for God meaningful to you?

Have you started thinking about how you will celebrate your little one's first year of life? For what are you most grateful?

Worthy

And they sang a new song, saying:
"You are worthy to take the scroll,
and to open its seals; for You were
slain, and have redeemed us to God
by Your blood out of every tribe and
tongue and people and nation."

REVELATION 5:9

Throughout this devotional we have contemplated the attributes of God from mercy to love to justice and patience. And sometimes we've seen how when we hold our babies in our arms, those little ones can remind us to behold the wonder of God for attributes like His creativity, generosity, and goodness. Hold and behold: that twofold act of wonder where attention to the gift leads us to praise the Giver. Through it all, we've examined God's manifold perfections like the facets of a diamond.

But one day, when time is a memory, we will worship together like nothing we have ever experienced. Redeemed and made new, we will sing a new song to our King. Nothing could be more right than to do so. He is worthy of all praise. Perhaps you've been to a wedding where the happy couple is toasted by their friends and family. Their praises are sung by long-time friends and family. Despite the couple's faults and imperfections, we still toast them and laud who they are. But in the world to come, we will praise the faultless One. Our gratitude will not be hampered by our sin, our joy will not be tempered by our suffering, our attention will not be diverted by our worries; we will sing a new song of unrestrained happiness as we worship a Savior who is totally and utterly worthy of our praise and adoration.

Not Worthy

I baptize you with water, but he who is
mightier than I is coming, the strap of
whose sandals I am not worthy to untie.

LUKE 3:16 ESV

$\mathcal{H}$ aving a baby is humbling. While you may have diplomas on your wall, when it comes to mothering, most of us begin as novices. As we blunder through the first year, it can be freeing to admit we are learning right along with our babies.

Likewise, the starting point for our relationship with Christ is our poverty. In the Sermon on the Mount, the poor in spirit, the meek, and those who hunger and thirst for righteousness are those blessed with the kingdom. That is why, here in Luke, John the Baptist—a holy man, the cousin of Jesus, and someone who has had the Holy Spirit in him since the womb (Luke 1:15)—can see Jesus and say of himself, "the strap of whose sandals I am not worthy to untie." Humility is the proper starting place for any relationship with Jesus. He is worthy; we are needy. He is holy; we are made holy by His sacrifice.

As you enter into the presence of God by prayer, enter as holy ones of the past have entered. Look at Jacob's prayer before he wrestled with God: "I am not worthy of the least of all the mercies . . . which You have shown Your servant" (Genesis 32:10). Or look at how the centurion asked for healing: "Lord, I am not worthy that You should come under my roof" (Matthew 8:8). This isn't false humility. This is a keen awareness of the holiness of God.

Walk Worthy

Only let your manner of life be worthy
of the gospel of Christ, so that whether
I come and see you or am absent, I may
hear of you that you are standing firm.
PHILIPPIANS 1:27 ESV

Perhaps your baby is army crawling these days or maybe even taking some first faltering steps. Or perhaps he will be a late bloomer, like so many of mine. Either way, I'm sure walking is top of mind as you near that first birthday. Repeatedly in Scripture, we are exhorted "to walk in a manner worthy of God, who calls you" (1 Thessalonians 2:12 ESV). While we are happy with whatever faltering first steps our babies take, we expect more from a mature adult. We expect a cadet in the US Naval Academy, for instance, to walk with shoulders back, chin level, back straight, and in step with others. More importantly, we expect the character of that cadet to be above reproach.

Wherever we go, we represent a company of much more distinction than the US Naval Academy. We represent Christ. Our words and actions should reflect the honor due His name. Walking worthy means standing firm for the faith, being of one mind, working side by side together for a cause bigger than ourselves: the gospel (Philippians 1:27). It means bearing fruit and growing in knowledge of God (Colossians 1:10). We carry His name with us as we go; let us ask God for the grace to represent Him well today. Let us walk worthy of the calling we have received.

You are not there yet, but even today, right where you are—on a nursery glider or on a coffee break at the office—close your eyes for a moment and imagine joining the chorus: "Worthy is the Lamb who was slain, to receive power and wealth and wisdom and might and honor and glory and blessing!" (Revelation 5:12 ESV). What do you think it will be like on that day to praise our worthy King?

Write a prayer for your baby to grow to be an adult who walks worthy of the gospel.

Victorious God

Do not be fainthearted or afraid; do not panic or be terrified by them. For the LORD your God is the one who goes with you to fight for you against your enemies to give you victory.
DEUTERONOMY 20:3–4 NIV

a s the Israelites prepared to enter the promised land, we see a refrain of "do not be afraid." While there was much to fear, God reinforced that He would fight their battles. He was on their side. He would give the victory. As they entered the land, God's reputation at the Red Sea preceded Him. The Amorite and Canaanite kings quaked in fear at the mere mention of the Israelites: "Their heart melted" (Joshua 5:1).

In the years that followed, God demonstrated time and again that He would give the victory. At Jericho, the Israelites defeated a mighty city merely by walking around it and blowing trumpets. This was God's doing! In Judges, Gideon sent home twenty-two thousand men of his army and ultimately defeated the Midianites with empty jars and torches. The victory clearly belonged to the Lord when a young shepherd boy named David defeated Goliath with a sling and a stone and faith in God. God wants us to see that He is the hero of our story: the victorious One— the One who wins the battle. As this first year with Baby comes to a close, you may feel anxious about whether you have what it takes for the road ahead. Remember like the Israelites not to be afraid and to keep looking to God, the strong One. He is the hero of your story and Baby's story, too, even of those pages yet to be written.

Lord of Hosts

Then she made a vow and said, "O
Lord of hosts, if You will indeed look
on the affliction of Your maidservant
and . . . give Your maidservant a male
child, then I will give him to the Lord."

1 SAMUEL 1:11

One of the names of God used frequently in the Old Testament is Lord of Hosts (Adonai Tzevaot or Jehovah Sabaoth). These names invoke His power and the hosts, or angel armies, at His disposal. They remind us that He is our warrior who will fight for us. It is interesting then to see this name in the middle of Hannah's prayer to be a mother. Hannah desperately wanted a child. She prayed so earnestly at the temple that the priest thought she might be intoxicated. Instead, she was pleading with God. And the name she chose to call God here was not the one used by Hagar (Jehovah Shema, the God who sees me) or by Abraham (Jehovah Jireh, the God who provides). Instead it was Adonai Tsevaot, or the Lord of Hosts. Why did this would-be mother call on the Lord of Hosts?

She appealed to the same God who defeated His enemies at the Red Sea to be her God and give victory over something that likewise was out of her control: her own fertility. What a beautiful window for us mothers to see how unafraid Hannah was to invite God into this intimate need. She trusted in His powers over the unseen realms. Where do you need the victorious Lord of Hosts today? Perhaps you, too, are beginning to pray for another child or have deeply personal needs where you need to see God bring victory. Whatever it is, you can trust Him with your heart.

Ultimate Victory and Celebration

And I heard . . . "Alleluia! For the Lord
God Omnipotent reigns! Let us be glad
and rejoice and give Him glory, for the
marriage of the Lamb has come, and
His wife has made herself ready."
REVELATION 19:6–7

As you near that one-year birthday milestone, I'm sure you are getting ready for a great celebration. You've made it through labor, sleep deprivation, and Baby's teething and tummy pains. You've seen your baby gain some mastery over his little body. It's been a grand year and one worth celebrating! We all love to have parties to celebrate victories. The Bible tells us that one day we will hear the victory announcement "Alleluia! For the Lord God Omnipotent reigns!" followed by the greatest celebration we've ever known: the marriage of the Lamb—a party to end all parties!

This will be a celebration of all the victories Christ has won, such as His victory over death (1 Corinthians 15:56–57) and over evil powers. As it says in Colossians 2:15, "And having disarmed the powers and authorities, he made a public spectacle of them, triumphing over them by the cross" (NIV). And we will celebrate His ultimate victory over the Evil one, for as Revelation says, "These will wage war against the Lamb, and the Lamb will overcome" (17:14 NASB). All the wonder-filled days we have known up until that point will pale in comparison to that final celebration. Truly, we will watch in wonder for all our days, beholding His glory face-to-face!

When we know a story ends with "happily ever after," it helps us relax and enjoy its ups and downs. How can God's ultimate victory give you peace today?

What "first" has your baby experienced lately? Which "firsts" are you looking forward to most?

God of Peace

Then the LORD said to him, "Peace be
with you; do not fear, you shall not die."
JUDGES 6:23

Research shows that babies as young as six months can sense the emotional state of their caregivers. If you are stressed, Baby can become stressed too. Touch, singing lullabies, and walking with Baby all have calming effects on your baby's emotional state.[1] But while a peaceful baby is a beautiful goal, when the Bible uses the word *peace*, it means much more.

Shalom, or peace, is a central concept in the Israelites' culture, and it means complete wholeness. It conveys an idea of a multidimensional flourishing. It is God's vision of well-being for humanity and reflects His wholeness, completeness, and perfection.

Shalom became for the Israelites a greeting—and here is its first use in this context. Gideon was astonished when he realized this was a message from God. He expected law and consequences from God. He received grace. Gideon was so moved by this that he built an altar of remembrance to God, calling it "The-Lord-Is-Peace," or shalom.

Our God of peace knows that our flourishing cannot coexist with sin, however. In Gideon's story the Israelites were worshiping Baal and being oppressed by the Midianites. That's why in the chapters that follow, the God of peace led Gideon into conflict. Only through ridding Israel of idolatry could she flourish. Likewise, the vision of shalom should lead us to battle against sin in our hearts. As we, by the Spirit, uproot envy, pride, and discontent, we make room for the flourishing God intends. God's shalom is worth fighting for.

A Farewell Blessing

Peace I leave with you, My peace I
give to you; not as the world gives do
I give to you. Let not your heart be
troubled, neither let it be afraid.

JOHN 14:27

The Upper Room Discourse (John 13–17) contains some of the most poignant words in the Bible. These words, this meal, these moments shared intimately here between Jesus and His disciples would be the last of their kind before everything changed. Nothing would ever be the same.

And these final lessons to them hearken back to the Old Testament. These are words of shalom—a promise of completeness and wholeness that He leaves with us. This peace is not a peace as the world gives. The world gives incomplete peace. The world offers peace that doesn't deal with the root of the problem. In the Old Testament, the prophet Jeremiah criticized the people for this, saying, "'Peace, peace!' When there is no peace" (Jeremiah 6:14). This kind of peace is not the shalom of Jesus. Jesus is bringing a total peace—the peace of reconciliation between man and God, procured at ultimate cost to Himself.

You are also at a moment of transition as your baby turns one. As the infant days recede and the toddler days arrive, you may feel anxious or sad. But Jesus' peace is for us in times of transition, in the unknown of what's ahead and in the wistfulness of what we leave behind. It is a peace that stretches and permeates past, present, and future if we will let it. Christ's peace for you amid change is every bit as real as it was for the disciples.

In the Light of His Face

The LORD bless you and keep you; the
LORD make His face shine upon you, and
be gracious to you; the LORD lift up His
countenance upon you, and give you peace.
NUMBERS 6:24–26

I chose the name of this book, *Watching in Wonder,* for a twofold purpose. While the first year with your infant is full of challenges, it is also full of so much wonder. As moms of very little ones, we do lots of watching as we hold that miracle. But I also chose this title because I hope this year has been one where, through this book, your face has not only been fixed on the face of your baby but also turned toward God—that, as you have studied His character each week, your delight in Him has grown. And as you continue to grow in Him, I pray that you will, in turn, be an ongoing source of blessing to your child, your family, and all those around you.

Today's scripture is a benediction or a blessing given to the people of God by the priests, and it fits so well with this book's theme. It is my prayer for you that His face may shine on you. This famous prayer asks for a threefold blessing: protection, pardon, and peace. May God protect you from evil and harm, be gracious to you (not giving you what your sins deserve), and give you peace, or shalom. This is a complete and perfect wholeness—a total, multidimensional flourishing. These blessings are wholly dependent on Him. They are not blessings man can bestow but blessings of the favor of God to you. And these, dear mother, are what I'm praying for you as you turn the page on another year of life with your little one and walk together into the wonder of all that is to come.

We don't have many verses about the childhood of Jesus. But we do have this one from Luke 2:52: "And Jesus grew in wisdom and stature, and in favor with God and man" (NIV). How can this picture of shalom guide you as you pray for your own little one's development? Remember shalom is a multidimensional picture of human flourishing.

Your baby is almost one! What are some of the moments you've cherished most in your first year with Baby?

Monthly Memories and Milestones

One unique thing about Baby is . . .

_____

_____

_____

Baby delights us when . . .

_____

_____

_____

_____

One thing I will miss most about this first year with my baby
is . . .

_____

_____

_____

_____

Something I'm excited about as this new chapter with my toddler begins . . .

Other moments or milestones from this month . . .

Happy Birthday!

How did you celebrate your little one's first birthday?

_____

_____

_____

_____

_____

_____

_____

_____

Who were the special people who joined in celebrating?

_____

_____

_____

_____

_____

_____

Did your little one receive any special gifts?

Did you have a cake or special food to celebrate?

What was your favorite moment?

An Invitation

If you've read this book and it has blessed you, I'd love to have you continue the journey with me in my next book, *Walking in Wonder*, a devotional journal like this one but for moms of toddlers. Also consider blessing another mother with this book or my book for expecting moms, *Waiting in Wonder*. What a wonderful way to come alongside a new mom and celebrate her and the wonder of that new baby!

For more of my writing and to check out my free gifts for new moms, visit my website at www.CatherineClaireLarson.com and friend my Facebook page or Instagram at Catherine Claire Larson. I pray that this book deeply enhanced both your life for Christ and the life of your child to the glory and praise of God.

Notes

Your Two-Month-Old, Week Four Theme: Patient
1. "Patience Is an Action Word," https://free.messianicbible.com/feature/patience-is-an-action-word/.

Your Three-Month-Old, Week Four Theme: Wise
1. "Infant Vision: Birth to 24 Months of Age," American Optometric Association, https://www.aoa.org/healthy-eyes/eye-health-for-life/infant-vision?sso=y.

Your Four-Month-Old, Week One Theme: Love
1. Christopher Bergland, "Early Maternal Love Boosts Child's Brain Growth," *Psychology Today*, May 2, 2016, https://www.psychologytoday.com/us/blog/the-athletes-way/201605/early-maternal-love-and-support-boosts-childs-brain-growth.

2. Sarah Sloat, "Brains Get a Boost from a Mom's Heartbeat," *Inverse*, https://www.inverse.com/article/44782-mothers-day-science-facts-attachment.

Your Six-Month-Old, Week Two Theme: Forgiving
1. "A Life in Sleep--How Sleep Plays Out over a Lifetime," Ergoflex.com, September 17, 2013, https://www.ergoflex.co.uk/blog/category/sleep-research/a_life_in_sleep_how_sleep_plays_out_over_a_lifetime?awc=17254_1649826158_dc807699ae8d17e7e0echa09d9312494&utm_source=aw&utm_medium=affiliate.

Your Six-Month-Old, Week Three Theme: Meek
1. Melissa Willets, "Babies Know When You're Angry and Want to Appease You," *Psychology Today*, March 24, 2016, https://www.parents.com/baby/all-about-babies/babies-know-when-youre-angry-and-want-to-appease-you/.

Your Nine-Month-Old, Week One Theme: Father
1. R. C. Sproul, "What Does It Mean for Us to Call God Our Father?" Ligonier, https://www.ligonier.org/learn/qas/what-does-it-mean-us-call-god-our-father.

Your Ten-Month-Old, Week One Theme: Redeemer
1. Rebecca Jackson, "Study Finds Habits in Children Take Root by Age of 9," *Psychology Today*, February 26, 2015, https://www.psychologytoday.com/us/blog/school-thought/201502/study-finds-habits-in-children-take-root-age-9.

Your Eleven-Month-Old, Week Four Theme: Peace
1. Gwen Dewar, "Stress in Babies: How to Keep Babies Calm, Happy, and Emotionally Healthy," Parenting Science, https://parentingscience.com/stress-in-babies/.

Feel the Comfort of God Each Day

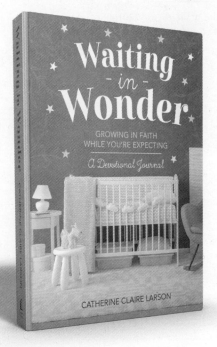

Pregnancy is an exciting time, and you don't want to forget a single moment of this journey. *Waiting in Wonder: Growing in Faith While You're Expecting* inspires you to record stories and prayers for your baby as you create a memory book you'll treasure for years to come.